How To...

PLAY SOLO UKULELE

BY CHAD JOHNSON

PLAYBACK+
Speed • Pitch • Balance • Loop

To access audio visit:
www.halleonard.com/mylibrary

Enter Code
4508-9183-3161-9118

ISBN 978-1-4950-6320-6

HAL•LEONARD®

7777 W. BLUEMOUND RD. P.O. BOX 13819 MILWAUKEE, WI 53213

Visit Hal Leonard Online at
www.halleonard.com

CONTENTS

ABOUT THE AUTHOR

Chad Johnson is a freelance author, editor, and musician. For Hal Leonard Corporation, he's authored over 80 instructional books covering a variety of instruments and topics, including bestsellers *Ukulele Aerobics* and *Guitarist's Guide to Scales Over Chords*, as well as *How to Record at Home on a Budget*, *Baritone Ukulele Aerobics*, *Ukulele Scale Finder*, *Pentatonic Scales for the Guitar: The Essential Guide*, *Ukulele for Kids*, and *Bass Fretboard Workbook*, to name but a few. He's a featured instructor on the DVD *200 Country Guitar Licks* (also published by Hal Leonard) and has toured and performed throughout the East Coast in various bands, sharing the stage with members of Lynyrd Skynyrd, the Allman Brothers Band, and others. He works as a session musician, composer/songwriter, and recording engineer when not authoring or editing. Chad currently resides in Denton, TX with his wife and two children. Feel free to contact him at *chadjohnsonguitar@gmail.com* with any questions or comments. To keep up with Chad's latest books and other musical projects, check out *www.facebook. com/chadjohnsonguitar*.

INTRODUCTION

The recent resurgence in the ukulele's popularity has been astounding. Websites like YouTube are simply overflowing with videos of folks strumming and singing their favorite songs on the uke. And uke videos in which virtuosos like Jake Shimabukuro and James Hill pull off dazzling solo versions of popular songs regularly reach views in the six and seven figures. Witnessing this phenomenon was the impetus of this book. While I can't promise that you're going to end up with the uke chops of Jake or James, I can provide you with fun and relatively painless ways to play your own solo versions of your favorite songs on the instrument.

How to Play Solo Ukulele is aimed at the intermediate ukulele player that already has a basic command of common chord shapes, simple strumming techniques, and rudimentary melodic playing. If any of these things are still beyond your grasp, I recommend practicing these things more thoroughly before attempting the material in this book. It's not that you won't be able to get anything out of it, but there will likely be concepts that are beyond your current skill level. Having a solid grasp of the aforementioned topics, however, will put you on firm footing for the material covered here. These arrangements are written for standard (soprano) or concert ukulele in reentrant tuning: G–C–E–A (with string 4 tuned to a high G). At times, the high G string is specifically used for melodic playing and certain chord voicings, so the arrangements in this book won't always clearly translate to the baritone ukulele or a tenor ukulele in low G tuning.

On many instruments, a solo arrangement can take myriad forms. Obviously, instruments that can only play one note at a time will be somewhat more limited than those, such as the uke, that can play several, but there are still countless ways to skin a cat in this regard. This book will cover arrangements in a range of difficulties, but the material presented throughout should prepare you well for the musical and technical challenges present in each and every arrangement.

The most enjoyable aspect of arranging songs for solo performance is that the process never gets old. Every song is different, and each one will present its own set of challenges and possibilities. But the rewards for putting in the work are well worth it, as the feeling of playing your own arrangements is tough to beat. I thoroughly enjoyed putting the material for this book together, and it's my hope that it provides you with valuable tools and insight on the subject. Consider any of the arrangements here as launching points that you can manipulate into something of your own. I'd love to hear from you in this regard and/or hear any of your own arrangements, so feel free to contact me.

Best regards,
Chad Johnson

HOW TO USE THIS BOOK

How to Play Solo Ukulele is basically divided into three main sections. Chapters 1–2 are designed to get everyone up to the same speed on the most important elements that we'll need for our arrangements, including basic pluck- and fret-hand techniques and chord/scale theory. Think of these as the minimal requirements for this book. So, if any of this is not second nature to you, I'd recommend working through it. Even if you're pretty sure you know all of this already, I recommend at least reading through it to make sure nothing sticks out. It'll also help to make sure you understand all the terminology I'm using in latter parts of the book, as not everything in this regard is standardized throughout the music and/or uke world.

Chapters 3–6 are the meat and potatoes of the book—the section where you'll really learn the ins and outs of creating a solo arrangement for ukulele. Lots of specific concepts are covered here—including chord inversions, melodic range, rhythmic adjustments and/or simplification, etc.—all of which can play a key role in almost any arrangement. Because each song is unique, this section will provide you with the know-how to make the adjustments, compromises, and alterations that are necessary to create an effective arrangement. There's no paint-by-numbers method that will work for every song, so it's important to develop versatility and a broad knowledge base to handle what comes your way. Needless to say, this section is mandatory reading and should not be skipped over by anyone.

Finally, in Chapter 7, we'll look at many arrangements of popular songs. These will range in style and difficulty and make use of all the concepts we've covered in the book. It's the payoff for all the work you've done. Once you master some—or all—of these arrangements, I encourage you to put your own spin on them. We all have our own aesthetic, and I'm sure my choices aren't always the ones you'd make. So think of the arrangements in this chapter as not only performance exercises, but also creative exercises in variation and embellishment. Try different textures (maybe strumming instead of fingerpicking), different harmonies (whether it's adding harmony notes to the melody or changing the chords beneath a melody), etc. This type of thing can be a whole lot of fun on its own, and the process can help you decide what you favor when creating brand new arrangements of your own.

Most of all, enjoy the process of working through this book. Hopefully, you'll learn lots of new things and demystify others. If you don't already make a habit of it, play your arrangements for your friends and family when you get them down. It's always fun to see and hear their reactions, and it's great practice if performing on stage is a goal of yours. Now get pluckin'!

ABOUT THE AUDIO

Most of the examples in this book can be found in the accompanying audio recordings. To access these, follow the directions on page 1 of this book. Refer to the audio when you have trouble understanding any of the concepts or simply when you need to hear how something is supposed to sound. Just like a picture, many times a recording can be worth a thousand words.

All examples performed by Chad Johnson
Recorded and mixed by Chad Johnson at Magnetized World Studio in Anna, TX

Before we can start cranking out arrangements of our favorite songs, we need to be able to understand how they were created. You can think of an arrangement of a song as a puzzle. The more you know about chord and scale construction, the easier the puzzle will be to put together. Know a little bit, and the edges of the puzzle become straight, which makes it considerably easier to get started. Know even more, and the pieces become bigger and more unique, which makes them much easier to fit together.

THE MAJOR SCALE

We'll begin with perhaps the most important bit of theory you'll ever learn: the *major scale*. This is the building block of Western harmony and has been for centuries. It, and its close cousin, the minor scale, are responsible for the melodies of literally millions of songs throughout the years, so it makes sense that we should familiarize ourselves with it.

INTERVALS

The first stop on the way to the major scale is the *interval*. This is simply the musical distance between two pitches; for example, from C to D is one type of interval, while from C to G is another type. Right now, we're only going to concern ourselves with two specific intervals: the *half step* and the *whole step*.

The half step is the smallest interval in Western music. On a piano, it's the distance from one key (black or white) to the very next key (black or white). On the uke, it's the distance of one fret on one string.

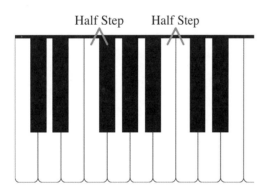
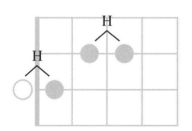

A whole step, as you may have guessed, is simply twice that of a half step. It's two keys on the piano and two frets on the uke.

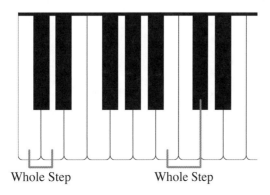
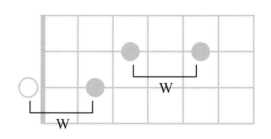

By the way, these two intervals go by other names, as well. The half step is also known as a *minor 2nd* (m2), and the whole step is also known as a *major 2nd* (M2). We'll see how those names come into play later on.

So, now that we know what a half step and whole step are, we have the power to build any major scale we want! It's quite exciting, really. How do we do it? Well, we simply follow our intervallic formula. Read on!

INTERVALLIC FORMULA

There are two major scale formulas that we'll look at in this book. The first of these is the *intervallic formula*. It's simply a specific order of half- and whole-step intervals that we use to construct a major scale. And here it is:

Whole–Whole–Half–Whole–Whole–Whole–Half

If you don't already know this, take a second and memorize it. And I don't mean that in the "memorize the capitals of South America for a test and then immediately forget it afterwards" way. I mean commit it to long-term memory. It's much easier than a bunch of capitals. Say it with me now: "Whole, whole, half, whole, whole, whole, half." Excellent!

What this means is that we can start on any note and, using this formula, build a major scale from that note. It could be F, A♭, E♭, C♯, whatever… as long as we follow this formula, we'll end up with the matching major scale. Let's check it out by using C as our tonic note.

C Major Scale

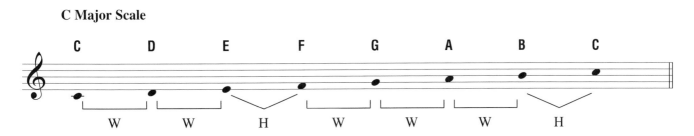

So, we can see that the C major scale contains no sharps or flats. Consequently, it's nothing but white keys on the piano. This is the only major scale like that. Every other major scale will include one or more sharps or flats (but never both). This is because there are two natural half steps in the musical alphabet: between B and C and between E and F. And in our major scale formula, we can see that the half steps fall between the third and fourth degrees and the seventh and eighth (or first in a new octave) degrees. This happens to be B/C and E/F in the C major scale, so no accidentals are needed. (For your information, the seventh degree of the major scale is called the *leading tone*, and it's crucial in tonic music, as it often helps us achieve a solid *cadence*, or resolution.)

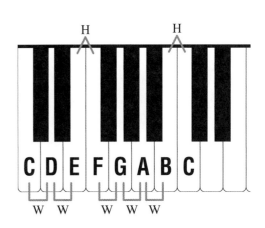

Now let's build a major scale from a different tonic to see how this will no longer be the case. We'll use the note G. To build any major scale, we can simply follow these steps:

1. **Write out the notes of the musical alphabet from the tonic to its octave.** Since we're using G as our tonic, it would look like this: G–A–B–C–D–E–F–G.

2. **Check the notes against the intervallic formula (W–W–H–W–W–W–H) to see where any discrepancies occur.** We can use the piano keyboard to do this because it's such a nice visual aid. If we place these notes on the keyboard, we can see that we have a problem toward the end of the scale:

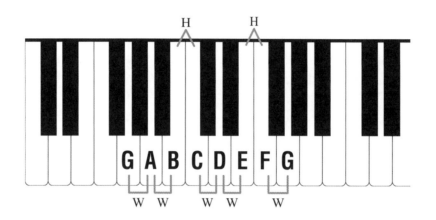

Instead of a whole step from the sixth to the seventh degree, we have a half step (from E to F). And instead of a half step from 7 to 8, we have a whole step (F to G).

3. **Make the necessary adjustments to the accidental(s) to right the formula.** The solution in this case is to raise F to F♯. By doing this, we correct both problems at once. We have a whole step from 6 to 7 (E to F♯) and a half step from 7 to 8 (F♯ to G).

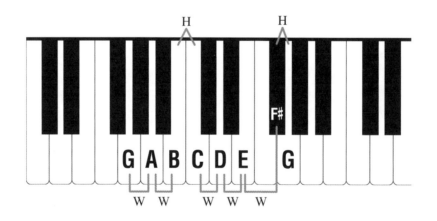

So, our G major scale is spelled G–A–B–C–D–E–F♯. Note that the "eighth" degree, G, is really just the first degree an octave higher. A major scale only has seven *different* notes in it. We usually include the tonic note in the higher octave, as well, so we can see the entire intervallic formula at work, but when "spelling" the scale (i.e., listing its notes), there's no need to include the tonic twice.

G Major Scale

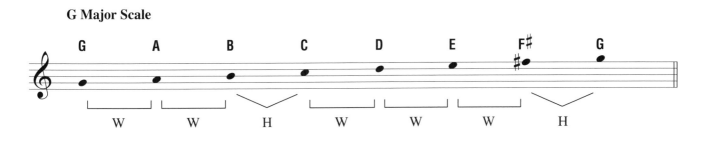

SPELLING IS IMPORTANT!

In our G major scale, we saw that we needed to add one accidental in order to maintain the intervallic formula. But how did we know to call the note F♯ instead of G♭? Those two notes are *enharmonic* (a term that means two different names for the same note), so why did we choose F♯? The answer is because a major scale must contain seven different letter names. In other words, *every letter of the musical alphabet, from A to G, must be present in every major scale.* This rule is without exception. Since we were building a G major scale, the letter G was already taken. If we called the accidental note G♭, then we would have two G notes and no F note. Therefore, we have to call it F♯.

For future reference, if you ever find yourself spelling a major scale and you end up with a letter being used twice, it's a red flag that you've made a mistake. And if one letter is being used twice, then another letter isn't being used at all (unless you've really gone astray and have eight different notes in your major scale or something!). This means that you most likely just need to use the enharmonic equivalent of one of the notes, and you'll fix the problem.

Let's try building another major scale, this time using the note F as our tonic. Repeating the steps outlined earlier, we first need to write out the letter names from tonic to octave:

F–G–A–B–C–D–E–F

Now let's check those notes against our intervallic formula on the piano keyboard:

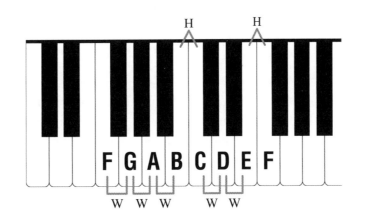

We can see that we have a problem with degrees 3 and 4 (A and B). We have a whole step between 3 and 4 instead of a half step, and we have a half step between 4 and 5 instead of a whole step. By lowering the fourth degree, B, a half step to B♭, we fix the problem.

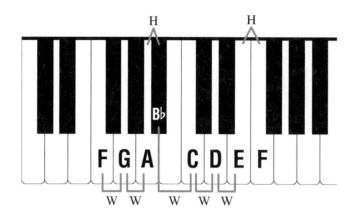

So the F major scale is spelled F–G–A–B♭–C–D–E.

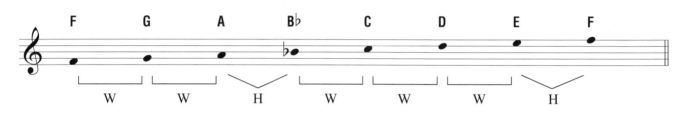

This helps illustrate that there are two types of keys: sharp keys like G major, and flat keys like F major. (I suppose there's a third type of key, as well, considering that C major contains no sharps or flats.) Just like the rule that each letter name needs to be represented in a major scale, there's another steadfast rule regarding accidentals: a major scale (other than C major) *will always contain either sharps or flats, but never both.* So, if you find yourself trying to spell a scale and you end up with a C♯ note and a G♭ note, you know you've made a mistake. Consequently, if you try to spell a major scale using both a sharp and a flat, you'll end up breaking the other rule (a letter name used twice), as well, so it should be obvious either way.

KEY SIGNATURES

Since we have flat and sharp keys, we use *key signatures* to make our lives easier with regard to reading music. The key signature will not only tell us what notes should be played as sharps or flats throughout the piece, but it will also tell us the key of the music. We've already demonstrated how to use our formula to build the G major and F major scale. If you continue this process for all 12 notes, you'll end up with 12 keys. The key signature is simply a listing of the sharps or flats contained within the key's major scale.

So, for example, since the G major scale contains an F♯, then its key signature is one sharp: F♯. Since an F major scale contains a B♭, its key signature is one flat: B♭. Using the intervallic formula to build the major scale from the tonic of each of the 12 keys is a great exercise, but I don't have the space to do that here. Instead, I'll just list all the key signatures and let you do the exercise on your own.

All 12 Key Signatures

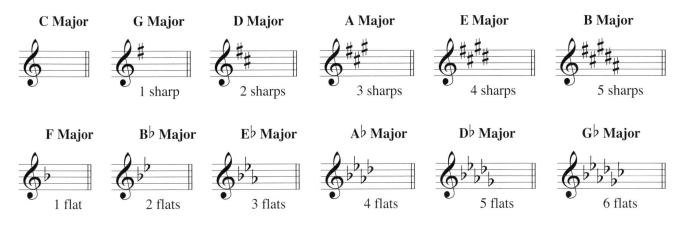

C Major	G Major	D Major	A Major	E Major	B Major
	1 sharp	2 sharps	3 sharps	4 sharps	5 sharps

F Major	B♭ Major	E♭ Major	A♭ Major	D♭ Major	G♭ Major
1 flat	2 flats	3 flats	4 flats	5 flats	6 flats

The 12 key signatures are often arranged in a circle diagram to help make memorizing them easier. This is called the *Circle of 5ths*, and it looks like this:

Circle of 5ths

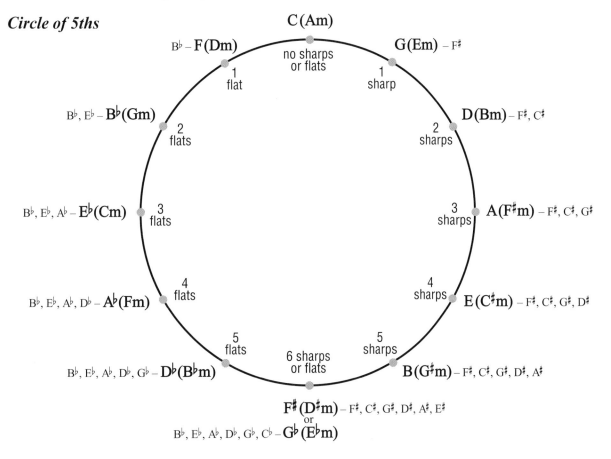

WHY IS IT CALLED THE CIRCLE OF 5THS?

The circle of 5th gets its name because, if you progress clockwise around the circle, each key is the interval of a 5th higher than the previous. Remember how we said that half steps and whole steps could also be called minor and major 2nds, respectively? This is because they are two letter names apart; for example, from C to D is a 2nd because it spans two letter names: C (1) and D (2). More specifically, it's a *major* 2nd because it's a whole step. From C to D♭ is a *minor* 2nd because it's only one half step. (We'll talk more about this later.) So, starting at the top of the circle, from C to G is a 5th because it spans five letter names: C (1)–D (2)–E (3)–F (4)–G (5). And, moving one more clockwise step around the circle, from G to D is another five letter names, and so on. Again, we'll talk more about intervals later on.

NUMERIC FORMULA

As mentioned earlier, aside from the intervallic formula (W–W–H–W–W–W–H), there's one other formula we'll look at for the major scale. This is the *numeric formula*. With this formula, we assign a number to each note of the scale. It doesn't seem particularly useful for a major scale at first, because the numeric formula for the major scale is simply:

However, this will help us greatly when building other types of scales and chords. It will also be useful when discussing chords, scales, and melodies in general. So, why do we assign numbers to the notes this way? Well, think of it this way: the major scale is the standard by which we measure other types of scales or chords. In other words, if you're in the key of C and you hear someone talking about the 3rd of the key, then you know they're talking about an E note because E is the third note in the scale (C–D–**E**–F–G–A–B). Or if you hear someone say, "The melody is in G major and goes 1–2–3–5," then you know that the melody is G–A–B–D because those numbers match up with those notes in the G major scale (**G–A–B**–C–**D**–E–F♯).

What's great about this, with regard to arrangements, is that it makes it very easy to transpose melodies. If you can describe a melody with numbers, then you can easily change keys by simply overlaying the numbers onto a different scale.

For example, let's say you have the same G–A–B–D melody as above and you want to transpose it to the key of B♭ major.

Well, first you assign numbers to the melody notes. As we saw above, the numbers for these notes are 1–2–3–5. Then you write out the scale in the new key (B♭ major) and add numbers to each note. Referring to our Circle of 5ths on page 11, we know that a B♭ major scale has two flats (B♭ and E♭), so it will look like this:

B♭	C	D	E♭	F	G	A
1	2	3	4	5	6	7

Now, compare the numerical melody to the notes in your new key, and you have it. So a 1–2–3–5 melody in B♭ major will be B♭–C–D–F. Easy!

Now try transposing the following C major melody to the key of A major.

The answer can be found at the bottom of the page (no peeking!). Remember the steps:

1. Assign numbers to the melody notes in the old key (C major). If necessary, write out the scale and number it.

2. Write out the scale in the new key (in this case, A major) and add numbers to each note.

3. Compare the numerical melody to the notes in your new key to find the transposed notes.

THE MINOR SCALE

Besides the major scale, the next most widely used scale in Western music is the *minor scale*. Whereas the major scale sounds happy and triumphant, the minor scale sounds sad, gothic, or dramatic. Since there are a few different types of minor scales, this is sometimes more specifically referred to as the *natural minor scale*.

INTERVALLIC FORMULA

The minor scale is another seven-note scale but with a different intervallic formula than the major scale. Instead of W–W–H–W–W–W–H, the intervallic formula for the minor scale is W–H–W–W–H–W–W. Let's take a look at the A minor scale to see how this works:

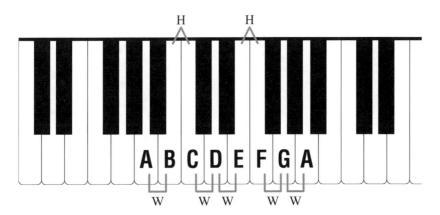

So, the A minor scale contains no sharps or flats. It's the only minor scale like that.

A Minor Scale

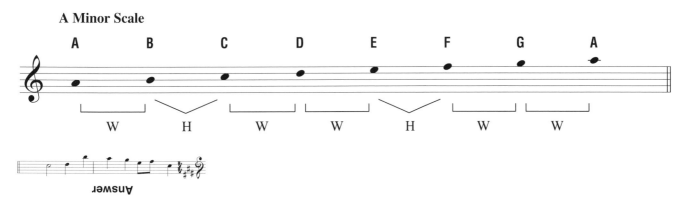

Answer

NUMERIC FORMULA

While the intervallic formula is a fine way to construct minor scales (the process is the same as for the major scales, only you use the minor intervallic formula), this is where the numeric formula really shines. Let's say we want to turn the C major scale into the C (natural) minor scale. Instead of starting over with the new intervallic formula for the minor scale, we can use the numeric formula for the minor scale, which is:

1   **2**   **♭3**   **4**   **5**   **♭6**   **♭7**

This means that, since the major scale is the "standard numeric formula" (represented simply by the numbers 1–7), we just need to alter the notes of the C major scale in the above fashion to create a C minor scale. So we take the C major scale, C–D–E–F–G–A–B, and we flat, or lower by a half step, the third, sixth, and seventh degrees. So we end up with:

C Minor Scale

It's easy to create any minor scale like this when you know the notes of the major scales. Let's look at converting the G major scale to the G minor scale. The notes of G major are G–A–B–C–D–E–F♯, and we just need to flat the third, sixth, and seventh notes. Remember: when we flat a note, we lower it by a half step. *This doesn't always mean we add a flat to a note.* It just means that we lower it by a half step. So, while the B and E notes of our G major scale will be lowered to B♭ and E♭, respectively, the F♯ note will simply be lowered to F.

G Minor Scale

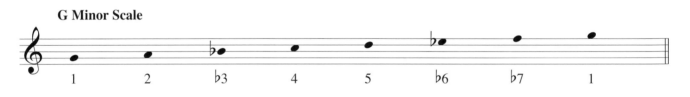

RELATIVE RELATIONSHIPS

Just as the 12 major keys had key signatures, so do the 12 minor keys. You may have noticed this on the Circle of 5ths diagram on page 11. Every major key signature is also the key signature of a minor key. At the top of the circle, we have no sharps or flats, which is the key signature for C major. But it's also the key signature for A minor. (If you remember from earlier, the A minor scale is the only minor scale with no sharps or flats.) These two keys, C major and A minor, have a *relative relationship* with each other. In other words:

- C major is the *relative major* of A minor

- A minor is the *relative minor* of C major

All 12 key signatures operate this way. So, G major is relative to E minor, D major is relative to B minor, and so on, all the way around the circle. This means that, when you see a key signature of one flat, for example, you don't necessarily know whether the song is in F major or D minor, but you know it'll be one of those. The context (chords, melody, etc.) will usually make it fairly clear, although it's not always black and white.

So, in summary, relative major and minor keys contain the same exact notes, but they have a different tonic (i.e., they treat a different note as the tonic).

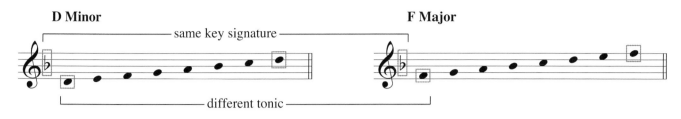

This type of relationship is present in lots of songs. A song may start in a major key and then shift to the relative minor for the bridge, for example, or maybe the chorus. The Beatles give us a fine example of this in "We Can Work It Out," which starts off in D major but then moves to the relative minor, B minor, for the bridge ("Life is very short, and there's no time…").

PARALLEL RELATIONSHIPS

The other type of relationship two keys can have is a *parallel relationship*. In this type, the two keys share the same tonic, but they have different notes. Our examples on page 14, in which we used the numeric formula to change C major and G major scales to C minor and G minor, respectively, are examples of a parallel relationship. In other words:

- C major is the *parallel major* of C minor

- C minor is the *parallel minor* of C major

This is not represented on the circle of 5ths, which demonstrates relative relationships, but it's a very useful songwriting or arrangement device. Like relative keys, it's very common for a song to start in one key and switch to its parallel key for a different section. It's more common to switch from major to parallel minor, but it does happen the other way around, as well. Again, we need look no further than the Fab Four for an example of this. "Norwegian Wood (This Bird Has Flown)" begins in E major (it's played in D on the guitar, but a capo at the second fret makes it sound in E) for the verse but then moves to E minor for the bridge sections.

So, in summary, parallel keys share the same tonic but contain different notes and therefore different key signatures.

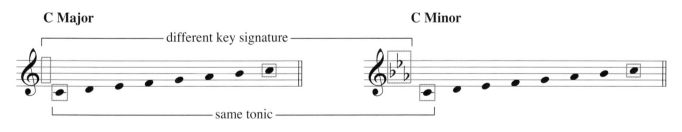

BORROWED CHORDS AND MODAL MIXTURE

It's often the case that, while a major song may not outright change to a parallel minor key, it will temporarily "borrow" chords and/or melody notes from the parallel minor. So, for example, we may have a song in C major that contains mostly chords from C major but borrows one or two chords from the parallel key of C minor. This type of thing, which is known as *modal mixture* (freely mixing of parallel major and minor tonalities) can help add sophistication and/or drama to a song. We'll look more at chords in the next chapter, but keep this in mind for future reference.

CHAPTER 2
CHORD THEORY PRIMER

Now that we all understand a good bit about scale construction, numeric formulas, and intervals, let's talk a bit about chord theory. Chords are usually three (or more) notes played together in harmonious fashion. When arranging songs, chords supply the harmony to the melody, so they're quite an essential part in our quest.

TRIAD CONSTRUCTION

The most popular type of chord is called a *triad*, so named because it's built from three different notes. These three notes are designated as the root (or "1st" as it relates to the other notes of the chord), 3rd, and 5th. The root note gives the triad its name. It is to the triad what the tonic is to the key. In other words, a C triad will have a C root, whereas an F triad will have an F root, and so on.

MORE ON INTERVALS

Since you're already familiar with the numeric-formula concept, building triads shouldn't be too foreign. Starting with the root note, the 3rd of the chord is—you guessed it—three letter names above the root. The 5th is five letter names above the root. So, to build a C chord, we need a C note (the root), an E note (the 3rd), and a G note (the 5th).

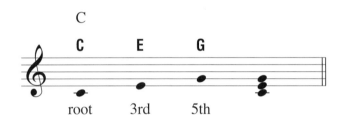

This happens to be a C *major* chord because of the specific intervals contained within it. Just as there are different types of 2nds—major and minor—there are different types of 3rds, 5ths, and every other kind of interval, as well. This is because each interval is comprised of two parts: a *quantity* and a *quality*.

The quantity is easy; all you do is count the letter names involved. In other words, from G up to C is a 4th because there are four letter names involved: **G** (1)–A (2)–B (3)–**C** (4). It doesn't matter if it's G♭ up to C♯, or G♯ up to C♮, etc. As long as the interval spans four letter names, it's *some kind* of 4th.

The quality gets more specific. There are five types of qualities used to describe intervals: *major, minor, augmented, diminished,* and *perfect*. The chart below shows the intervals for all 12 notes of the octave measured against a C root note. This may look intimidating, but there's logic behind it.

Notes	# of half steps	Interval name	Abbreviation
C to C	0	Unison	P1
C to D♭	1	Minor 2nd	m2
C to D	2	Major 2nd	M2

Notes	# of half steps	Interval name	Abbreviation
C to E♭	3	Minor 3rd	m3
C to E	4	Major 3rd	M3
C to F	5	Perfect 4th	P4
C to F♯ C to G♭	6 6	Augumented 4th Diminished 5th	A4 d5
C to G	7	Perfect 5th	P5
C to A♭	8	Minor 6th	m6
C to A	9	Major 6th	M6
C to B♭	10	Minor 7th	m7
C to B	11	Major 7th	M7
C to C	12	Octave	P12

From this chart, we can deduce a lot about interval qualities. Here are some of the axioms on display:

1. **A minor interval is one half step *smaller* than its major-interval companion.**

    C to E (four half steps) = major 3rd

    C to E♭ (three half steps) = minor 3rd

2. **An augmented interval is one half step *larger* than its perfect-interval companion.**

    C to F (five half steps) = perfect 4th

    C to F♯ (six half steps) = augmented 4th

3. **A diminished interval is one half step *smaller* than its perfect-interval companion.**

    C to G (seven half steps) = perfect 5th

    C to G♭ (six half steps) = diminished 5th

4. **The terms "major" and "minor" do not apply to 4ths and 5ths.** We use "perfect," "augmented," or "diminished" to describe them.

5. **The term "perfect" does not apply to 2nds, 3rds, 6ths, or 7ths.** We use "major" or "minor" to describe them, although "diminished" and "augmented" are occasionally used, as well. We can, at times, have augmented 2nds and 6ths, which are one half step larger than major 2nds and 6ths, respectively. We also, at times, see a diminished 7th interval, which is one half step smaller than a minor 7th.

ENHARMONIC INTERVALS

You'll notice that both F♯ and G♭ are listed, even though they are the same note. The term for a note having two different names is *enharmonic* (e.g., F♯ and G♭ are enharmonic to each other). Don't get confused by enharmonic intervals. Always remember the rule of the interval's *quantity*! For an interval to be called a 2nd, there *must* be *two* note names involved. For an interval to be a 6th, there *must* be *six* note names involved, etc.

For example, what's the interval from C up to E♭? Well, we know it's some kind of 3rd because there are three note names involved: C (1), D (2), and E♭ (3). And we know that it's a *minor* 3rd because it's three half steps in distance (this is confirmed in the previous chart).

However, what about the interval from C to D♯? The notes E♭ and D♯ are enharmonic; they're the same note. But the interval from C to D♯ is technically *not* a minor 3rd. Why? Because of the quantity rule! There are only *two* note names involved: C (1) and D♯ (2). We know that from C to D is a major 2nd, and since C to D♯ is one half step larger than a major 2nd, we call it an *augmented* 2nd (A2). It will sound just like a minor 3rd, and if you heard it, you'd probably call it a minor 3rd, as that label is much more common. But there are instances when it will make sense to write it as C to D♯, instead of C to E♭, and in those instances, it's technically considered an augmented 2nd.

Although we used flat names for all the accidental notes in the chart, we can name the other intervals with sharp notes as well.

C to C♯ is technically an augmented unison (A1), C to G♯ is an augmented 5th (A5), and C to A♯ is an augmented 6th (A6).

FOUR TRIAD TYPES

Now let's get back to the topic of building chords. There are four types of triads that we can create with a root, 3rd, and 5th: major, minor, augmented, and diminished (don't confuse these names with the interval names that we just talked about).

MAJOR TRIAD (1–3–5)

A *major triad*, like the major scale, is the happiest-sounding of the bunch. Its chord symbol simply consists of an uppercase letter. So, if you see the chord symbol "C," it indicates a C major chord. The specific intervals contained in the chord, respective to the root, are as follows:

- **Major 3rd (M3):** Distance of four half steps (or two whole steps)

- **Perfect 5th (P5):** Distance of seven half steps (or three-and-a-half steps)

 TRACK 1

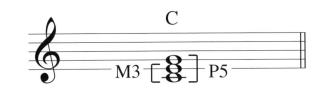

The tonic chord (triad built from the tonic note) in any major key is always a major chord. Listen to Track 1 to hear this triad played on piano.

MINOR TRIAD (1–♭3–5)

A *minor triad*, like the minor scale, is sad and dramatic. Its chord symbol is represented with an uppercase letter followed by a lowercase "m" suffix. The chord symbol for a C minor triad, for example, is "Cm."

The specific intervals contained in the chord, respective to the root, are as follows:

- **Minor 3rd (m3):** Distance of three half steps (or one-and-a-half steps)

- **Perfect 5th (P5):** Distance of seven half steps (or three-and-a-half steps)

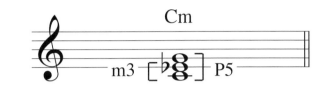

The tonic chord (triad built from the tonic note) in any minor key is always a minor chord. Track 2 contains a Cm triad.

AUGMENTED TRIAD (1–3–♯5)

An *augmented triad* sounds somewhat spooky or mysterious. Its chord symbol is represented by an uppercase letter with a "+" sign suffix. So, "C+" indicates a C augmented chord. The specific intervals contained in the chord, respective to the root, are as follows:

- **Major 3rd (M3):** Distance of four half steps (or two whole steps)

- **Augmented 5th (A5):** Distance of eight half steps (or four whole steps)

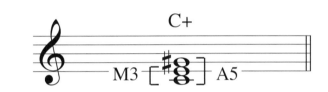

The augmented triad does not normally appear in a major or minor key by default; you have to use accidentals to create one. Though nowhere near as common as major and minor chords, augmented triads do show up on occasion. Listen to Track 3 to hear a C+ chord.

DIMINISHED TRIAD (1–♭3–♭5)

A diminished triad is very eerie-sounding and is often used to create lots of tension, as it sounds very unresolved. Its chord symbol is represented by an uppercase letter with a "°" symbol suffix. So, "C°" indicates a C diminished triad. The specific intervals contained in the chord, respective to the root, are as follows:

- **Minor 3rd (m3):** Distance of three half steps (or one-and-a-half steps)

- **Diminished 5th (d5):** Distance of six half steps (or three whole steps)

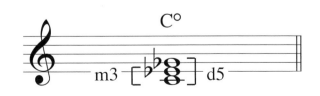

In a major key, the triad built from the seventh degree is a diminished chord. Listen to Track 4 to hear a C° chord.

THE HARMONIZED MAJOR SCALE

As mentioned earlier, we can build a triad off each note in a major scale. Since there are seven notes in the scale, there are seven different triads contained within it. When we build a chord from each note, we say we are *harmonizing* the scale.

To do this, we first write out the notes of a major scale. We'll use C major here:

Now, treating each note as the root, we follow the process we did earlier: add a note that's a 3rd above and another that's a 5th above each root. The first chord is built on the tonic of the key, which is C, and we know from our previous studies that it's a C major chord and is "spelled" C–E–G.

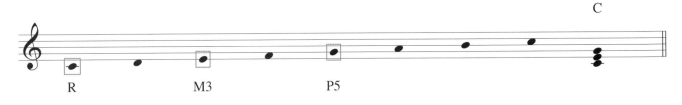

The next chord is built off the second note of the scale, D. A 3rd above D is the note F, and a 5th above D is the note A (remember that the musical alphabet simply starts over after we reach G). This is a minor triad, Dm, and it's spelled D–F–A.

How do we know it's a minor triad? Well, we can look at the intervals. From D to F is three half steps (you can verify this on a piano keyboard), so it's a minor 3rd. From D to A is seven half steps, so it's a perfect 5th. A minor 3rd and a perfect 5th from the root make a minor triad.

When we repeat this process for every note of the scale, we end up with the triads notated below. Similar to the numeric formula for scales, we use Roman numerals to indicate the chords and their *quality* (major, minor, etc.). Uppercase Roman numerals are used for major chords, while lowercase are used for minor chords (augmented is indicated by an uppercase numeral followed by "+," and diminished is indicated by a lowercase numeral followed by "°").

Here then are all seven diatonic triads in C major:

🔊 **TRACK 5**

Harmonized C Major Scale

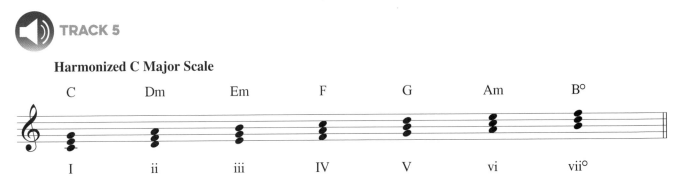

Just as every major scale follows the intervallic formula of W–W–H–W–W–W–H, the harmonized major scale also follows a formula. The harmonized scale always contains the following triad types, regardless of the key:

I	ii	iii	IV	V	vi	vii°
major	minor	minor	major	major	minor	diminished

As noted earlier, the only triad of the four different types not to appear in the diatonic major scale is the augmented triad, which can only be created with some type of accidental.

If we harmonize another major key, we'll end up with seven different chords, but the order of the qualities will still be the same (major–minor–minor–major–major–minor–diminished). Let's check out the harmonized G major scale. Note that we'll shift down an octave half way through to make them all playable on the uke.

 TRACK 6

Harmonized G Major Scale

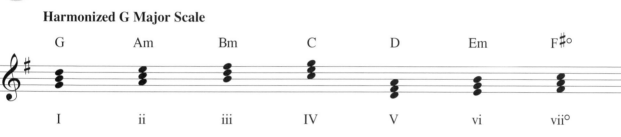

THE HARMONIZED MINOR SCALE

Harmonizing the minor scale works the same way: you treat each note as a root and add a 3rd and 5th above it from the scale. We'll get a different formula for the order of chord qualities but, again, every minor scale will adhere to it. Let's check out the A minor scale.

 TRACK 7

Harmonized A Minor Scale

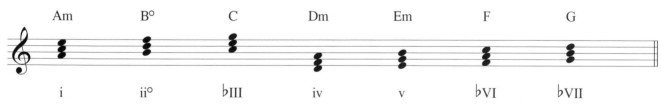

So, the triad formula for the minor scale is:

i	ii°	♭III	iv	v	♭VI	♭VII
minor	diminished	major	minor	minor	major	major

Note also how the Roman numerals mirror the numeric formula of the minor scale:

i	ii°	♭III	iv	v	♭VI	♭VII
1	2	♭3	4	5	♭6	♭7

Again, we can do this with another minor key to see that, although the chords will change, the order of qualities won't. Here's the same thing in the key of E minor:

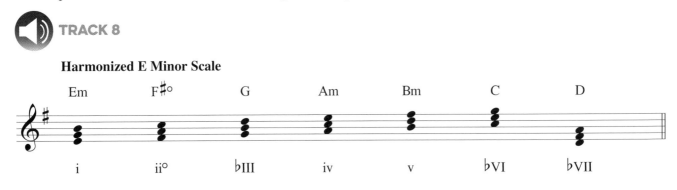

Coincidentally, you may have noticed that the order of the qualities here is the same as in the major scale, only it's shifted over (to the right) by two chords. When you overlay them, you can see this:

Major Key:	vi	vii°	I	ii	iii	IV	V	vi	vii°
	minor	diminished	major	minor	minor	major	major	minor	diminished
Minor Key:	minor	diminished	major	minor	minor	major	major	minor	diminished
	i	ii°	♭III	iv	v	♭VI	♭VII	i	ii°

This is the relative relationship at work again. In other words, since C major and A minor share the same key signature, you could call a Dm chord a ii chord in C major or a iv chord in A minor (and, if all you had was that Dm chord and a blank key signature—no sharps or flats—you wouldn't know which one is really correct).

REVIEW

Before we proceed, let's go over what we've learned thus far to make sure everyone is up to speed.

- Every scale has an **intervallic formula** of half steps and whole steps. For the major scale, this is W–W–H–W–W–W–H, and for the minor scale, it's W–H–W–W–H–W–W.

- A **key signature** tells you what notes will be performed as sharps or flats throughout the piece. There are 12 key signatures. A blank key signature indicates C major or A minor. Every other key signature will either be a flat key or a sharp key.

- The **Circle of 5ths** arranges the 12 keys in a circle whereby each key moves up by an interval of a 5th as you progress clockwise. At the top of the circle (12:00) is C major/ A minor, and at the bottom (6:00) is F♯ major/D♯ minor (or, enharmonically, G♭ major/ E♭ minor). Both of these latter keys have six accidentals in their key signature.

- Every scale has a **numeric formula**, as well. The major scale is the standard, so it's simply 1–2–3–4–5–6–7. The minor scale's numeric formula is 1–2–♭3–4–5–♭6–♭7.

- A **half step** (also known as a minor 2nd) is the smallest interval in Western music. It's the distance of one key (white or black) on a piano or one fret on the uke. A **whole step** (also known as a major 2nd) is two half steps—two keys on the piano or two frets on the uke.

- The seventh note of a major scale is called a **leading tone**.

- **Enharmonic** notes sound the same but are spelled differently. The notes G♭ and F♯ are enharmonic.

- **Relative keys** share the same notes but have different tonics. C major (C–D–E–F–G–A–B) and A minor (A–B–C–D–E–F–G) are relative keys.

- **Parallel keys** share the same tonic but contain different notes. C major (C–D–E–F–G–A–B) and C minor (C–D–E♭–F–G–A♭–B♭) are parallel keys.

- The act of mixing notes or chords from parallel keys is called **modal mixture**.

- Any interval contains two parts: a **quantity** and a **quality**. The quantity is measured solely by counting letter names; for example, from D to F is a 3rd: D (1)–E (2)–F (3). The quality is measured by counting half and/or whole steps (see chart on page 16–17).

- A **triad** consists of three notes: a root (1), a 3rd (3), and a 5th (5). There are four types of triads that we can create with these notes: major (1–3–5), minor (1–♭3–5), augmented (1–3–♯5), and diminished (1–♭3–♭5).

- The **harmonized major scale** produces a set of triad types that always follows the same order: major, minor, minor, major, major, minor, diminished.

- We use **Roman numerals** to identify chords within a key. Uppercase numerals are used for major, and lowercase are used for minor. A "+" symbol added to an uppercase numeral is used for an augmented chord (which does not *naturally* occur in a major or minor key), and a "○" symbol added to a lowercase numeral is used for a diminished chord.

- The order of chords in any harmonized major scale using Roman numerals is: I–ii–iii–IV–V–vi–vii○.

- The order of chords in any harmonized minor scale using Roman numerals is: i–ii○–♭III–iv–v–♭VI–♭VII.

If any of these points are still not clear to you, please go back and review the material before proceeding. It's important to understand this information before moving on. With that said, it's time to start playing some songs.

Song arrangements can range in style and difficulty, but you have to start somewhere, and that's what this chapter is all about. We're just going to get our feet wet here with playing melodies and filling out things very sparsely at times. But the important thing is that we'll be playing recognizable songs instead of just strumming the uke (not that there's anything wrong with that!).

NOTATION PRIMER

We'll be including *tab* with the notation for all the musical examples in this book. In case you don't already know how to read it, it's very simple. There are four horizontal lines representing the four strings on the uke. The G string (string 4) is on the bottom, and the A string (string 1) is on top.

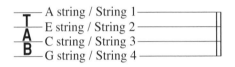

The numbers on these lines tell you which frets to play and on what string(s). A "0" indicates an open string.

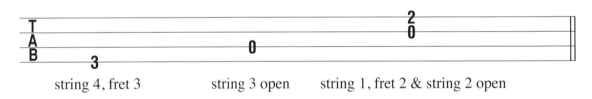

| string 4, fret 3 | string 3 open | string 1, fret 2 & string 2 open |

Although this will tell you specifically where to play a certain note on the uke (as you may know, you can often play the same note at several different places on the neck), it won't tell you anything about rhythm. That's where the notation comes in!

So, first thing's first. Let's start by simply playing some melodies to well-known songs in (or very near) *open position*. This means we'll be sticking to within about the first five frets. In case you don't know the notes on the uke neck, here are the names of the notes near open position:

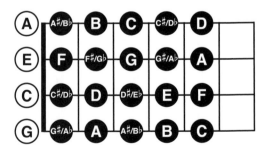

All right, let's dig in.

Please Please Me

Words and Music by John Lennon and Paul McCartney

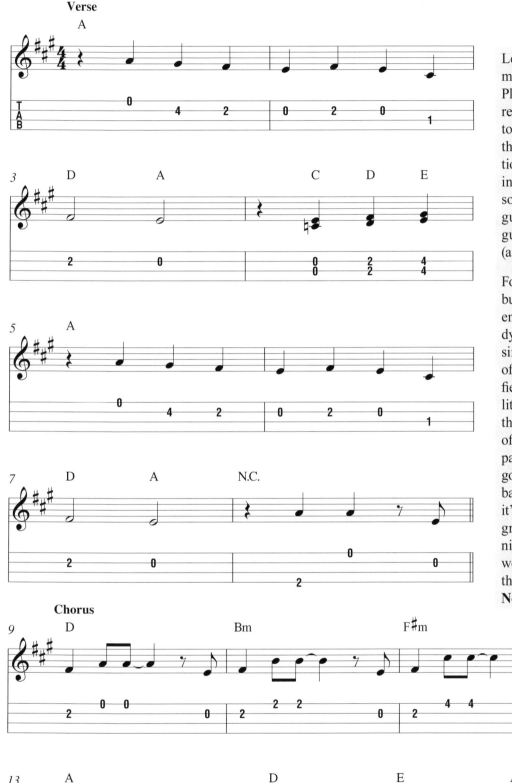

Let's begin with the verse and chorus melody to the early Beatles hit "Please Please Me." Although the original recording is in E, we'll transpose it to the key of A so that it sits nicely on the uke. You'll find that this transposition—i.e., up a perfect 4th (from E to A in this case)—will often work well for songs that were originally played on guitar because the uke is tuned like the guitar's top four strings, only up a 4th (and with string 4 up an octave).

For the most part, we're playing nothing but the melody here. However, after the end of the first vocal phrase, we play dyads for the chords that fill in the gaps since we would have a whole measure of rest otherwise. We've also simplified things rhythmically, omitting the little vocal ornaments and playing the chords as quarter notes instead of eighth notes. Also, during the first part of the chorus ("Come on…"), we go ahead and include the answering backup vocal melody as well, since it's easily done. Although the background vocal part is actually harmonized here on the original recording, we've omitted the harmony note so that we can remain near open position. **Note:** "N.C." stands for "no chord."

Scarborough Fair

Traditional English

Next up is the traditional folk song, "Scarborough Fair." I've arranged this one in D minor for the uke, as the melody falls quite nicely in open position. Since this is an old, *old* folk song, there are many variations of it in circulation. The melody and chords I've used here represent those used in what I feel are the most commonly heard versions of this song (although you may disagree with me!).

Again, we're mainly sticking to the melody for this 3/4 song. However, during the breaks between the vocal phrases, I've taken the opportunity to add some fingerpicked arpeggios to help maintain some interest. This type of thing is very subjective, and there's plenty of room for variation with regards to the arpeggio pattern, chords used, etc. Notice in measure 14 how we make creative use of the high G string for the Csus4 arpeggio. Also take note of measure 18; we're using the same arpeggio line that appeared earlier in measure 4. This helps lend a sense of continuity to the arrangement.

Ring of Fire

Words and Music by Merle Kilgore and June Carter

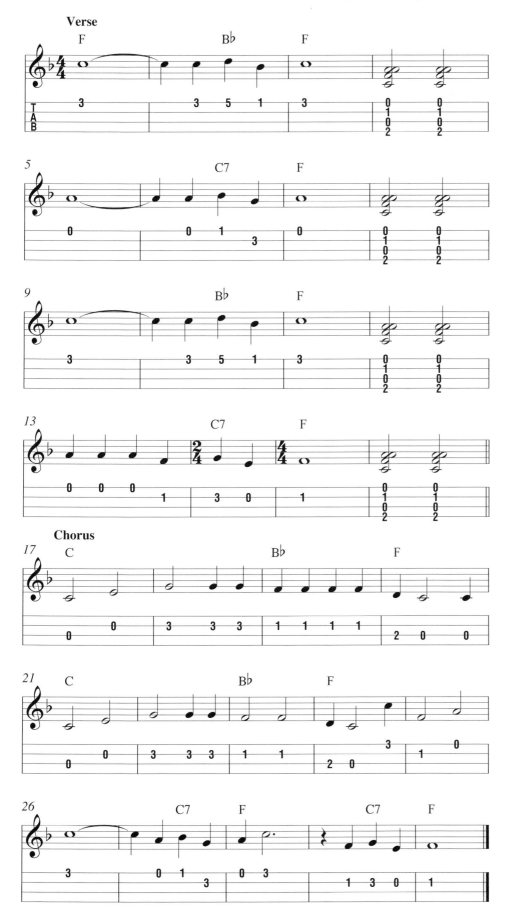

Here we'll take a look at the Johnny Cash classic, "Ring of Fire." The original recording begins in the key of G major and ends up modulating to several different keys before all is said and done, but we've transposed to F major here with no modulations. This song is a great example of the melody range issues that crop up at times. The original spans from a low 7th degree up to a high 2nd an octave up, or an octave and a 3rd. Because of the way it's situated within the key, if we want to stay within the first five frets of the uke, we can't keep it all in the original octave it appears. (If we put it in the key of D♭, we could fit it within the first six frets, but we're really trying to stay as close to open position as possible here.) So this means we're going to need to transpose a phrase (or phrases) by an octave. Also note that we've streamlined and simplified a few other elements as well, including the melody and most of the 2/4 measures that appear in the verse. We've filled in a few of the breaks with some half-note chord strums to keep the arrangement moving.

After some experimentation, I decided to use the key of F and begin in the upper octave for the verse. This means that when the chorus arrives (on the V chord, C), we have to bring the melody down an octave if we want to stay in open position. Of course, there's no law that says we have to stay in open position, but we're doing that as an exercise in these first arrangements just to get our feet wet. Notice in measure 24 that I decided to move back up to the high octave for the final note in the measure because this will help more accurately depict the motion of the melody on the original song, in which it falls from the 5th to the tonic on the lyric, "And it burns…"

Into the Great Wide Open

Words and Music by Tom Petty and Jeff Lynne

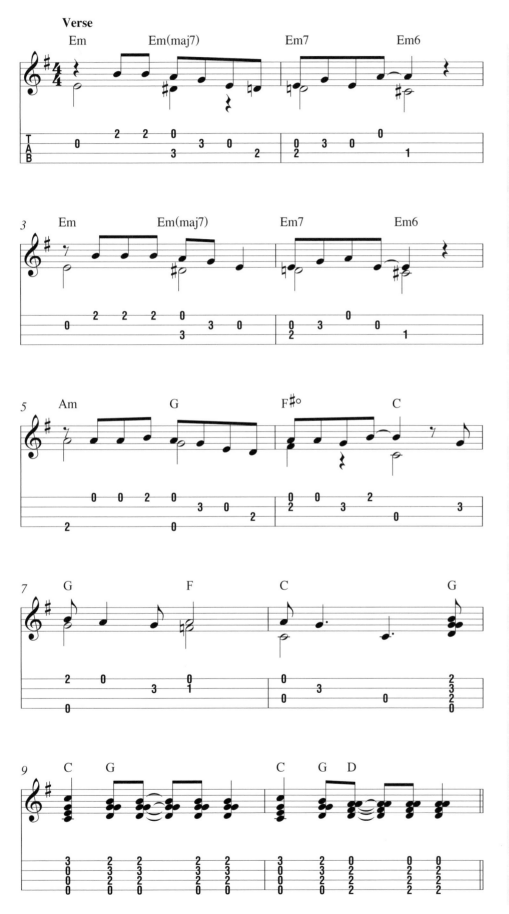

We'll finish off this chapter with Tom Petty's "Into the Great Wide Open." This will be our most ambitious arrangement thus far, as we'll be including bass notes with our melody, and we'll play it in the same key as the original recording: E minor (the chorus is in the relative key of G major). The notation includes two voices; play the downstemmed notes with the thumb and the upstemmed notes with the fingers. There are two new chords here that we haven't looked at thus far:

- **Em(maj7):** This is read "E minor major 7," and it's just like an Em7 except that it contains a major 7th interval instead of a minor 7th. It is spelled E–G–B–D♯.

- **Em6:** This is just like an Em triad with an added major 6th interval. It is spelled E–G–B–C♯.

Notice that these chords are used to create a chromatic bass line of E–D♯–D–C♯.

At the end of each section, we're strumming some chords to mimic the chord riff in the original recording, albeit with a simplified rhythm. If the rhythms are a bit tricky to get down, just listen to the audio track to clear up any problem spots. In the measures of the chorus where we have D chords, we play a little alternating pattern (fingers and thumb) that hints at a Dsus4 chord before returning to D. A "sus4" chord (short for *suspended* 4th) is a triad in which the 3rd of the chord (it could be a major or minor 3rd) is replaced with the 4th. It's very often used as a decoration (as is the case here) that's alternated with a major or minor chord. Dsus4 is spelled D–G–A.

Chorus

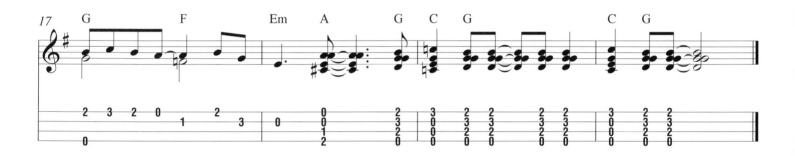

CHAPTER 4
MOVEABLE CHORD SHAPES AND INVERSIONS

The ukulele has a fairly limited range when compared to a guitar, or especially a piano, and that often means that we'll need to make use of the entire neck at times. Therefore, it's important to have a lot of chord grips under our fingers. In other words, we need to know how to play the same chord all over the neck. To do this, we'll use different inversions and voicings based on *moveable fingerings* (i.e., ones that don't contain open strings).

TRANSFORMING OPEN MAJOR CHORD FORMS INTO MOVEABLE ONES

In case you don't already know, just about any moveable chord is based off one of several open chord shapes. So, our first step is to simply turn these open chords into moveable ones. Some of these will most likely already be familiar, but they'll all prove useful at one point or another.

THE C CHORD

The open C chord is one of the easiest chords to play on the uke because it only uses one finger.

🔊 **TRACK 13**

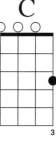

In order to turn this into a moveable chord, we just need to treat the nut as a finger barre. First, fret the open C chord with your pinky on string 1, fret 3 and your first finger barring the strings behind the nut (indicated with parentheses).

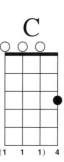

Now, if we slide that shape up two frets (one whole step), we get a D chord in moveable C Form.

🔊 **TRACK 14**

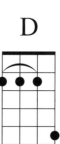

This is the essence of every moveable chord shape—seeing the nut as a barre (or sometimes just a single fretted note) and re-fretting the open chord without using your index finger. Then you simply slide that shape up the fretboard and replace the nut with your index finger to create the moveable shape.

THE A CHORD

The A chord barre form is another commonly used one. Here's the open A chord:

 TRACK 15

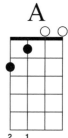
A

Now use your ring and middle fingers to re-fret that chord, laying your index finger down as a barre behind the nut. There's your barre form.

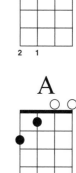
A

Slide that shape up two frets and you have a B chord in moveable A Form.

 TRACK 16

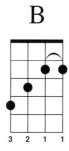
B

THE G CHORD

The open G chord is commonly fretted with fingers 1–3.

 TRACK 17

G

To make the moveable form, you'll need to re-fret it with fingers 2–4 and then lay the index finger on string 4 behind the nut.

G

Slide this form up a whole step and you have an A chord in moveable G Form.

 TRACK 18

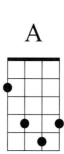
A

THE F CHORD

The open F chord looks like this:

 TRACK 19

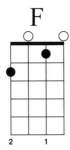

Re-finger it with the ring and middle fingers, laying the index behind the nut to act as a barre.

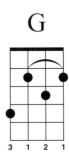

There's your moveable shape. Slide that up a whole step, and you have a G chord in moveable F Form.

 TRACK 20

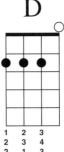

THE D CHORD

The D chord is one of the more difficult chords to finger for those with hands on the larger side. There are several fingering possibilities for it.

 TRACK 21

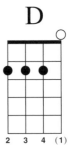

To play the moveable version of this chord, you have two choices: 1) you can use fingers 2–4, with your index finger on string 1 behind the nut, like this:

Or, 2) you can barre strings 4–2 with your ring finger and place you index finger behind the nut on string 1.

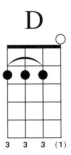

Move those fingerings up a whole step, and you'll have an E chord in moveable D Form.

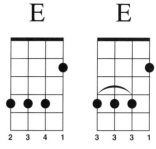

Most likely, not everyone will be able to use the barred third-finger method. However, I will say that the actual moveable version of this barred chord (as opposed to the one in open position in which your index finger is acting as a fake fret behind the nut) is easier because the first string is being pressed down, as well. In the open version, your ring finger barre has a harder job of clearing string 1, which is not being fretted and therefore is sitting higher off the fretboard. So, before you give up, try the moveable version (the E chord in second position) first.

LOOK FAMILIAR?

It's important to note the overlapping of these chord shapes when you can. For example, the open D Form should look very familiar to you, particularly on strings 4–2. Check out the moveable C-Form D chord on page 30 to see what I mean.

Taking note of these overlaps will help you piece together the notes on the entire neck.

PIECES OF A PUZZLE

Armed with these five moveable forms—C, A, G, F, and D—we can map out the entire neck by playing the same chord at different places. Let's check it out with a C chord. From low to high, we have five different C chord voicings:

- Open C chord (C Form)
- A Form
- G Form

- F Form
- D Form

TRACK 23

Take some time to really understand the connections here, and practice playing up and down the neck with different chords to make sure you've really got it. Depending on which chord you choose and/or which form you start with, you may have to move up or down an octave at some point.

Here's the same thing with a B♭ chord, starting with the moveable A Form in first position:

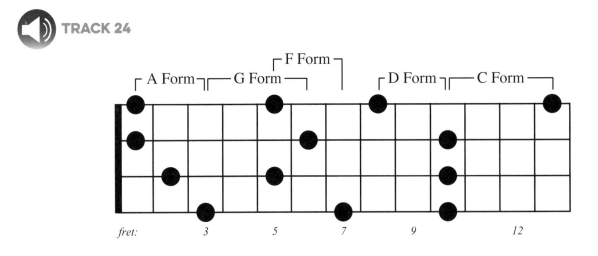

TRACK 24

TRANSFORMING OPEN MINOR CHORD FORMS INTO MOVEABLE ONES

Now let's do the same for the minor chords. There will be a few differences here and there, but it's the same exact concept. Since we know the process now, we can breeze through these pretty quickly.

THE Am CHORD

Here's the open form:

TRACK 25

And here's the moveable form up two frets, which results in a Bm chord in moveable Am Form:

TRACK 26

THE Dm CHORD

Here's the open Dm chord:

TRACK 27

And here's that form slid up two frets for an Em in moveable Dm Form:

TRACK 28

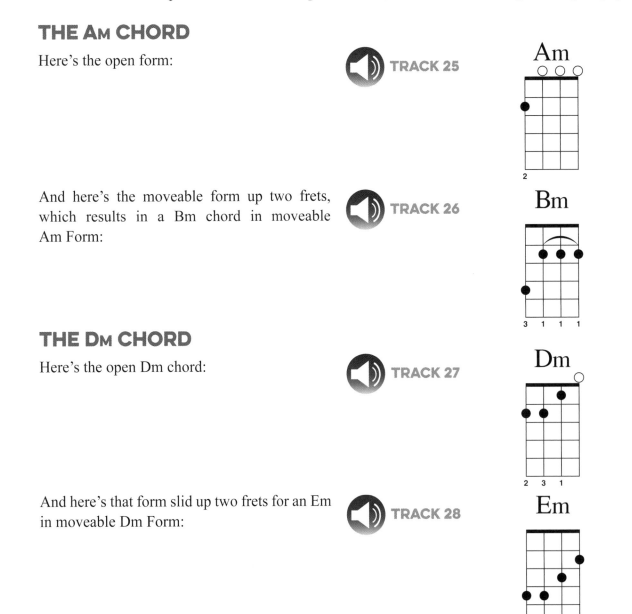

THE Gm CHORD

Here's the open Gm chord:

 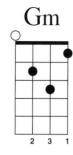

Moving that up two frets gives us an Am chord in moveable Gm Form:

 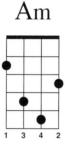

THE F♯m CHORD

The open F♯m chord looks like this:

 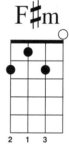

Moving that up two frets gives us a G♯m in moveable F♯m Form:

 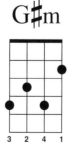

OTHER FORMS

The four previous forms represent the main moveable minor forms we'll use. Technically, there are a few others, but the moveable forms just end up being variants of others that we've seen.

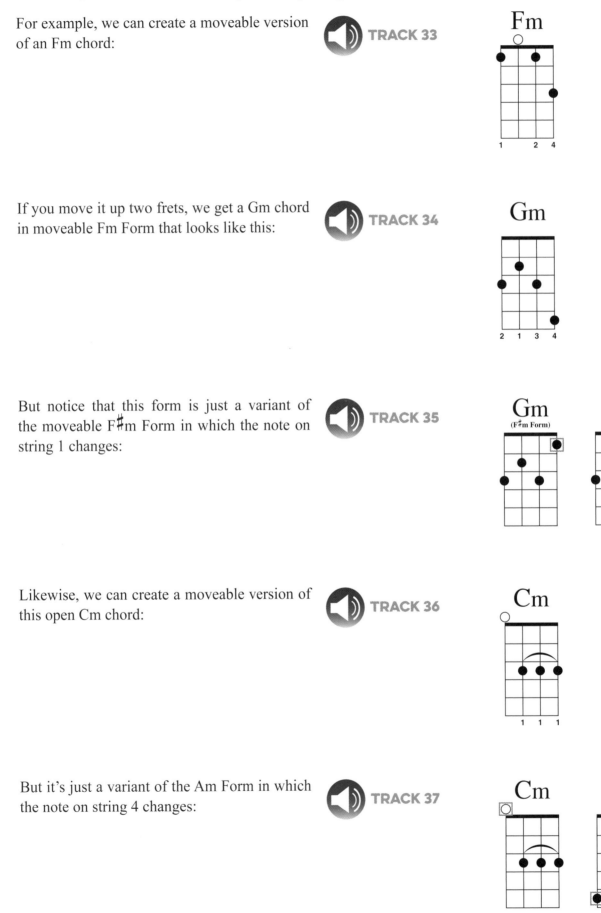

For example, we can create a moveable version of an Fm chord:

TRACK 33

Fm

If you move it up two frets, we get a Gm chord in moveable Fm Form that looks like this:

TRACK 34

Gm

But notice that this form is just a variant of the moveable F♯m Form in which the note on string 1 changes:

TRACK 35

Gm
(F♯m Form)

Gm
(Fm Form)

Likewise, we can create a moveable version of this open Cm chord:

TRACK 36

Cm

But it's just a variant of the Am Form in which the note on string 4 changes:

TRACK 37

Cm

Cm

INVERSIONS

To really reap the benefits of these chord shapes, we need to know exactly what's going on with each one (i.e., we need to know how each note functions within the voicing). This shouldn't be too difficult as long as you've worked through the theory chapters.

In order to be systematic about this, we'll look at three-note triad voicings—in other words, ones that contain only a root, 3rd, and 5th, with no double notes. On other four-stringed instruments, there would be more sonic possibilities in this regard because you could play chords on strings 4–2 *and* strings 3–1. However, the high-G tuning on the fourth string of the uke means that these two possibilities will sound the same. If this sounds confusing, don't worry—it will soon be clear.

Adjacent Voicings

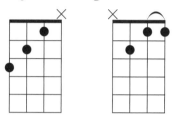

So let's take a look at these triads and how they lay out on the neck. There are two main categories that we'll look at: *adjacent voicings* and *non-adjacent voicings*. In an adjacent voicing, all of the notes will be on adjacent strings. In other words, they're either on strings 4–2 or strings 3–1.

Non-Adjacent Voicings

In non-adjacent voicings, one string will be skipped. So these will either be on strings 4, 3, and 1 or on strings 4, 2, and 1.

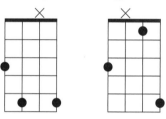

ROOT-POSITION MAJOR TRIAD (1–3–5): ADJACENT

The first voicing we'll look at is root position. This simply means that the root note is on bottom. Low to high, it's root–3rd–5th. For consistency, we'll look at all of these chords with a C root. Of course, these forms can easily be moved anywhere on the neck to play other chords, as well. And since you now know how to turn open chords into moveable forms, those forms won't present an obstacle, either.

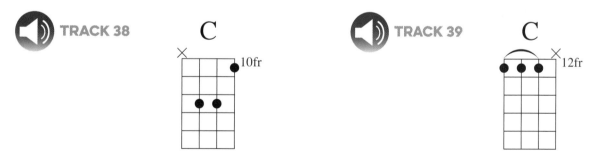

So now you can see and hear what I was talking about earlier. Because of the reentrant tuning, these two voicings sound the same due to the same octave being produced on both string 1 and string 4. Granted, they don't sound exactly the same, because the note on string 1 will generally "speak" a bit better than the one on string 4, and the order of the notes will obviously change if you're playing an arpeggio, but the point is that it's the same three notes in the same exact octave. We can (and will) use this to our advantage when arranging songs because often one of them will make better sense in the overall phrase.

FIRST-INVERSION MAJOR TRIAD (3–5–1): ADJACENT

In a first-inversion chord, the 3rd is on the bottom. It's as if we had the root-position chord and then just moved the root up an octave. As a result, it's 3rd–5th–root, low to high. On the uke, we'll move the whole thing down an octave and play this chord in third position.

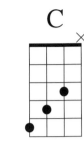

TRACK 40

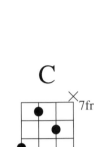

SECOND-INVERSION MAJOR TRIAD (5–1–3): ADJACENT

For the second inversion, we continue the process of moving the bottom note up an octave. We end up with the 5th on the bottom: 5–1–3.

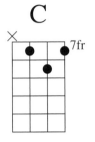

TRACK 41

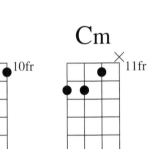

ROOT-POSITION MINOR TRIAD (1–♭3–5): ADJACENT

Now let's do the same with Cm triads. First up is root position.

TRACK 42

FIRST-INVERSION MINOR TRIAD (♭3–5–1): ADJACENT

For the first-inversion Cm chord, we'll again move down to the lower octave.

TRACK 43

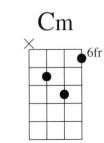

SECOND-INVERSION MINOR TRIAD (5–1–♭3): ADJACENT

The second-inversion Cm chord looks like this:

TRACK 44

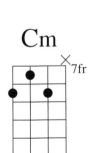

To save space in the book, we won't work through the augmented and diminished triad shapes individually, but you can find all of those voicings by making the appropriate adjustments to the major or minor triads. Now let's move on to the non-adjacent voicings.

ROOT-POSITION MAJOR TRIAD (1–5–3): NON-ADJACENT

Note that the lowest note in the chord is going to either be on string 3 or string 2 here since the fourth string is tuned to a high G.

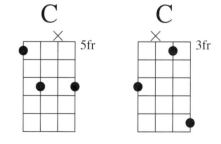

FIRST-INVERSION MAJOR TRIAD (3–1–5): NON-ADJACENT

Here are the first-inversion shapes:

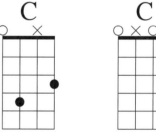

SECOND-INVERSION MAJOR TRIAD (5–3–1): NON-ADJACENT

And here are the second-inversion shapes:

ROOT-POSITION MINOR TRIAD (1–5–♭3): NON-ADJACENT

Here are the non-adjacent minor shapes. Again, remember that the lowest-sounding pitch is going to be on string 3 or string 2.

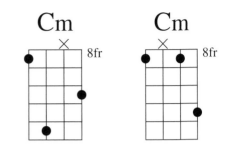

FIRST-INVERSION MINOR TRIAD (♭3–1–5): NON-ADJACENT

Here, the 4–3–1 shape is played in open position, whereas the 4–2–1 shape is played in the higher octave.

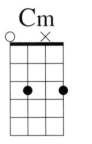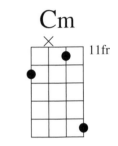

SECOND-INVERSION MINOR TRIAD (5–♭3–1): NON-ADJACENT

Many of these shapes can be fingered different ways. For example, the 4–2–1 shape could be played with your ring, index, and pinky fingers or your middle, index, and ring fingers. It's a good idea to try all the possibilities because one may work better than the other at some point in an arrangement.

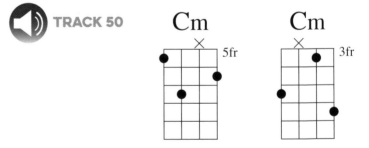

SEVENTH CHORDS

Now let's take a quick look at *seventh chords*, as they will commonly show up in many songs, as well. With your knowledge of triad construction under your belt, seventh chords should be a snap. Seventh chords are four-note chords that contain a root, 3rd, 5th, and 7th. Just as with triads, there are many types that we can create, depending on which type of 3rd, 5th, or 7th we use. Here are the formulas for the most commonly used seventh chords, shown here with a C root:

Major Seventh (1–3–5–7): A Cmaj7 chord is spelled C–E–G–B

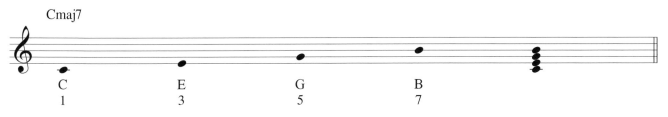

Minor Seventh (1–♭3–5–♭7): A Cm7 chord is spelled C–E♭–G–B♭

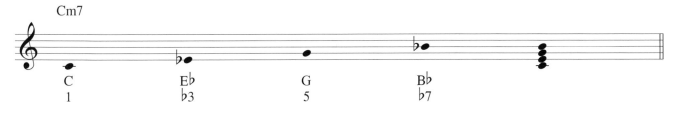

Dominant Seventh (1–3–5–♭7): A C7 chord is spelled C–E–G–B♭

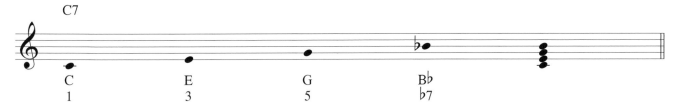

Minor Seventh Flat-Five (1–♭3–♭5–♭7): A Cm7♭5 chord is spelled C–E♭–G♭–B♭

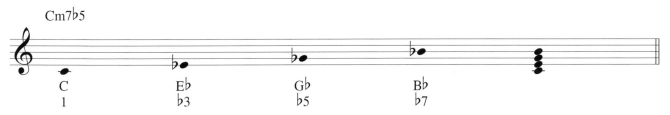

Diminished Seventh (1–♭3–♭5–♭♭7): A C°7 chord is spelled C–E♭–G♭–B♭♭ (B♭♭ is enharmonic to A)

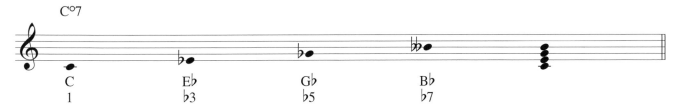

It's important to note the triads contained within these seventh chords; for example, major seventh and dominant seventh chords both contain a major triad (1–3–5) as their foundation. A minor seventh chord contains a minor triad (1–♭3–5). The minor seventh flat-five and diminished seventh chords both contain a diminished triad (1–♭3–♭5) as their foundation. The different seventh degrees further delineate them.

THE DIMINISHED SEVENTH ENIGMA

Don't be scared by the ♭♭7th in the diminished seventh chord. This note will sound the same as a major 6th interval; that is, from C to B♭♭ will sound the same as from C to A. It's a distance of nine half steps either way you name it. But it's technically called a B♭♭ in a C°7 chord because it's functioning as a ♭♭7th, and, remembering our quantity rule about intervals, if it's called some kind of 7th, seven letter names have to be used.

In practice, however, this is one of the times where the "rule" will be broken rather often. The reason for this is that a diminished seventh chord is a *symmetrical chord*; it's comprised solely of minor 3rd intervals stacked on top of each other. Check it out with our C°7 chord:

- From C to E♭ is a minor 3rd (three half steps).
- From E♭ to G♭ is a minor 3rd (three half steps).
- From G♭ to B♭♭ (A) is a minor 3rd (three half steps).
- From B♭♭ to C is technically an augmented 2nd because there are only two letter names used, but it's still three half steps (i.e., a minor 3rd).

Because of this, *any* note of the chord could be considered the root. So, C°7 could also be named:

- E♭°7 (or D♯°7)
- G♭°7 (or F♯°7)
- B♭♭°7 (or, more likely, A°7)

This chord's function is as chameleon-like as its name, and it's often used to change keys. It's basically used like a vii° triad, but it will sound even more uneasy. And since it functions like a vii° chord, you can pick any note to be the root and move up a half step for resolution. So, that same C°7 chord could resolve to four different chords:

- C°7 to D♭ (or B♯°7 to C♯)
- D♯°7 (or E♭°7) to E
- F♯°7 (or G♭°7) to G
- A°7 (or B♭♭°7) to B♭

Food for thought when you need a key change!

Now that we've learned how they're made, let's check out the seventh chord shapes and their inversions. Since these are four-note chords, we'll need all four strings to play them. Therefore, each chord will have only four possible voicings: root position, first inversion, second inversion, and third inversion (7th in the bass).

TRACK 51 • MAJOR SEVENTH (1–3–5–7)

Root Position

Cmaj7

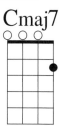

First Inversion

Cmaj7

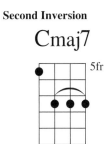

Second Inversion

Cmaj7

5fr

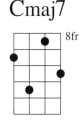

Third Inversion

Cmaj7

8fr

 TRACK 52 • MINOR SEVENTH (1–♭3–5–♭7)

Root Position

Cm7

11fr

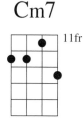

First Inversion

Cm7

Second Inversion

Cm7

5fr

Third Inversion

Cm7

8fr

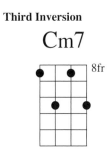

TRACK 53 • DOMINANT SEVENTH (1–3–5–♭7)

Root Position

C7

First Inversion

C7

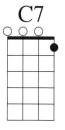

Second Inversion

C7

5fr

Third Inversion

C7

8fr

TRACK 54 • MINOR SEVENTH FLAT-FIVE (1–♭3–♭5–♭7)

Root Position

Cm7♭5

11fr

First Inversion

Cm7♭5

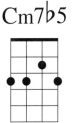

Second Inversion

Cm7♭5

5fr

Third Inversion

Cm7♭5

8fr

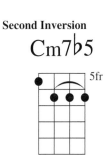

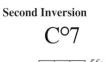

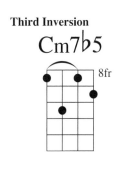

TRACK 55 • DIMINISHED SEVENTH (1–♭3–♭♭5–♭7)

Root Position

C°7

11fr

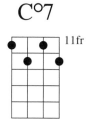

First Inversion

C°7

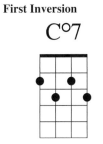

Second Inversion

C°7

5fr

Third Inversion

C°7

8fr

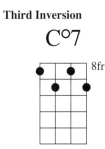

CHAPTER 5
TECHNICAL CONSIDERATIONS

Aside from learning different chord shapes all over the neck, there are some technical challenges that arise, as well, when playing solo ukulele, especially if all you've done thus far is strum. In this chapter, we'll take a look at the most common tools you'll need in your bag of tricks to handle most arrangements.

SCALAR PLAYING

We learned all about how to build scales in Chapter 1, and now it's time to play them. If you don't have any practice playing single notes, it will take a while to build up the coordination, so don't get discouraged.

MAJOR SCALE SHAPES

We'll start with the major scale. There are two main major scale shapes that we'll look at: 1) tonic on the third string, and 2) tonic on the second string. In open position, these will be the C major scale (tonic on the third string) and the F major scale (tonic on the second string).

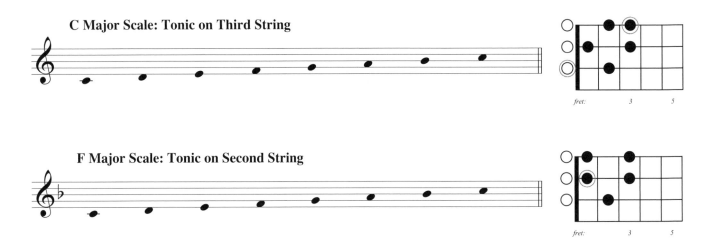

We can easily create moveable forms of these scales by moving each up the neck. Here's the same set of scales a whole step higher, resulting in moveable forms for D major and G major.

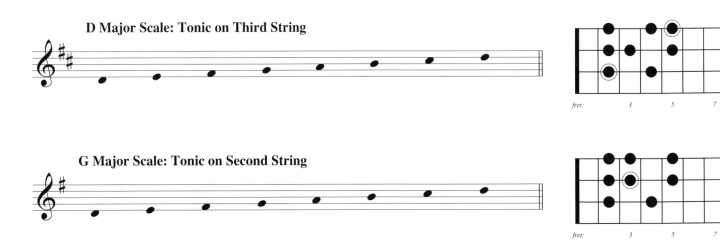

Now let's check out how it looks when both scale shapes are illustrated on the neck for the same root. Here are both C major scale shapes: the open-position shape with the tonic on string 3, and the seventh-position shape with the tonic on string 2.

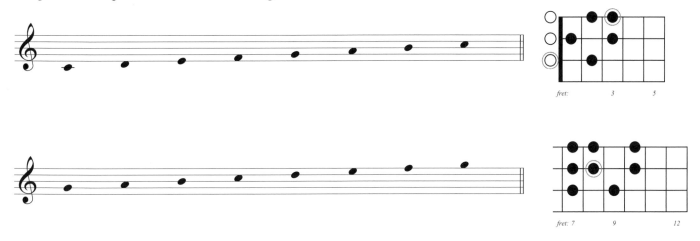

So, as you can see, there's only an area of a few frets between each scale position. Most likely, you can stray from these shapes briefly as needed in an arrangement, using these two as your "home base" when playing melodies. There are always exceptions, however, and there's no substitute for knowing the entire neck cold.

MINOR SCALE SHAPES

Now let's check out some useful minor scale shapes. We'll also present these in two forms.

C Minor Scale: Tonic on Third String

F Minor Scale: Tonic on Second String

And here's how it looks on the neck with both minor scale forms in C minor:

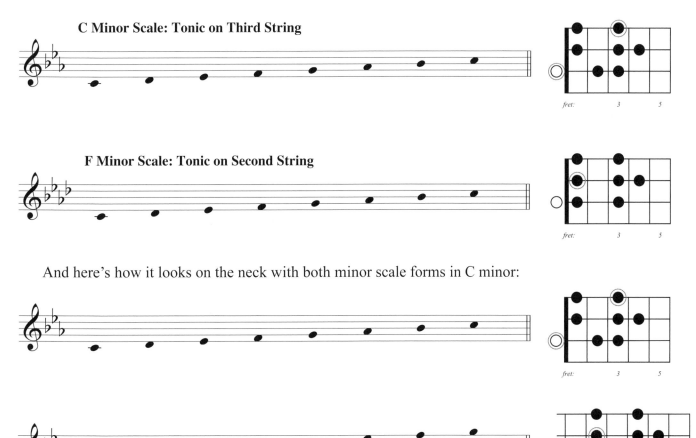

Having a command of these scale shapes will put you in good shape to handle most melodies that come your way.

WHAT ABOUT THE FOURTH STRING?

You'll notice that these shapes don't include the fourth string. This is because, within a scale form, the notes available on the fourth string already exist on the second and first strings. However, this isn't to say that we won't ever make use of it for melodies in our arrangements. But it will usually be done on an as-needed basis.

Now let's look at some exercises that will help get your chops up to the task.

SCALAR EXERCISES: PLUCKING

In these exercises, we'll pluck every note. There are numerous approaches you can use here for the pluck hand:

- Alternating index and middle fingers

- Alternating thumb and index (or middle) finger

- Alternating thumb strokes (works best if you have a decent bit of thumbnail)

- Any combination thereof

The method you choose will often depend on the particular phrase (tempo, difficulty, etc.), and no one method is better or more proper than the other. Jake Shimabukuro often makes use of alternating thumb strokes for his faster lines, whereas you can see James Hill make use of alternating index and middle fingers in some of his jazz arrangements. Like I said, it really depends on the arrangement. I'd recommend trying the following examples with various pluck-hand approaches, but I would suggest trying to get fairly comfortable with at least one method.

Our first two examples will use the open-position C major scale.

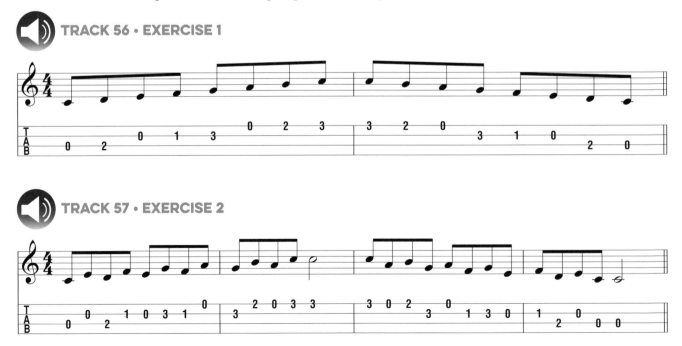

TRACK 56 • EXERCISE 1

TRACK 57 • EXERCISE 2

Now let's move up to the seventh-position C major scale. You'll get some good practice rolling your fret-hand fingers on this one.

TRACK 58 • EXERCISE 3

Now let's check out some C minor scale examples. This first one is a triplet sequence.

TRACK 60 • EXERCISE 5

Now let's move up to the seventh-position C minor scale.

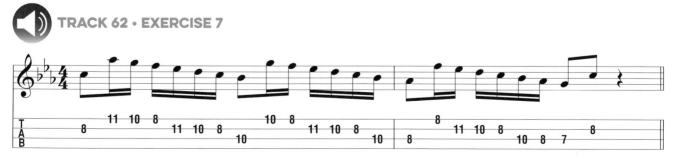

TRACK 62 • EXERCISE 7

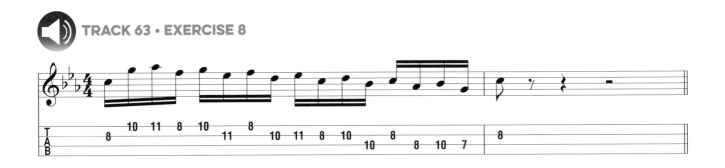

Now let's check out some pentatonic variations. To make a C major scale a C major pentatonic scale ("penta" meaning "five"), we simply leave out the fourth and seventh degrees, resulting in C–D–E–G–A. Here, then, are the two C major scale shapes in pentatonic form:

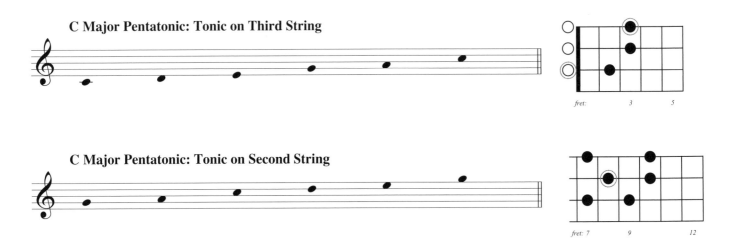

C Major Pentatonic: Tonic on Third String

C Major Pentatonic: Tonic on Second String

To create a minor pentatonic, we leave out the 2nd and ♭6th degrees of the minor scale. So, C minor pentatonic is spelled: C–E♭–F–G–B♭. Here, then, are the two C minor scales in pentatonic form:

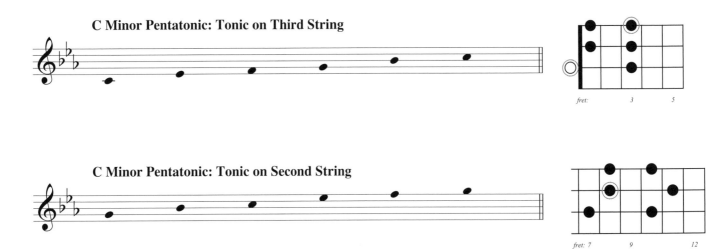

C Minor Pentatonic: Tonic on Third String

C Minor Pentatonic: Tonic on Second String

SCALAR EXERCISES: HAMMER-ONS, PULL-OFFS, AND SLIDES

Now let's play some pentatonic exercises. For these exercises, though, we're going to be making use of some hammer-ons, pull-offs, and slides to ease the burden on our plucking hand and to produce a more legato tone.

To perform a *hammer-on*, simply pluck a note (open or fretted) and then use a fret-hand finger to sound a higher note on that same string by forcefully "hammering" down onto the fret instead of plucking it.

🔊 TRACK 64

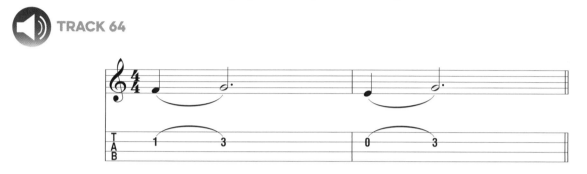

A *pull-off* is kind of the opposite. Pluck a higher note and then "pull off" to a note that's already fretted at a lower pitch (or an open string) on the same string. When you pull off, instead of just lifting your finger up and off the string, pull it downward quickly (toward the floor) so that you're essentially "plucking" the string with that fret finger.

🔊 TRACK 65

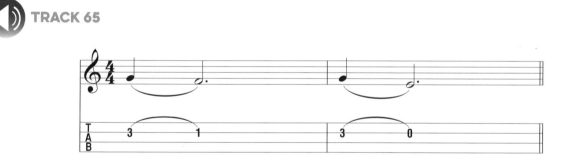

For a *slide*, pluck a fretted note and then slide that fret-hand finger up or down to another fret on that same string, being sure to maintain pressure while sliding. The destination pitch can either be plucked or not plucked.

🔊 TRACK 66

Here are a few examples from C major pentatonic:

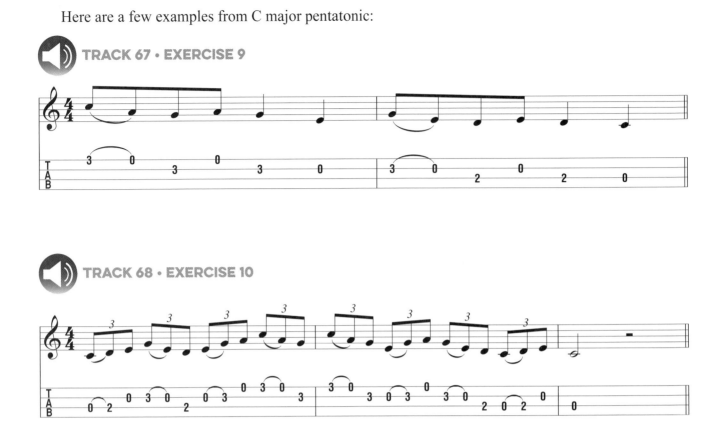

TRACK 67 · EXERCISE 9

TRACK 68 · EXERCISE 10

Now let's move up to the seventh-position C major pentatonic.

TRACK 69 · EXERCISE 11

TRACK 70 · EXERCISE 12

Now let's make use of some slides in C major pentatonic. For these examples, we'll use slightly different scale shapes to facilitate the slides.

Now let's make use of the C minor pentatonic scale shapes, first using hammer-ons and pull-offs.

And here are the altered forms of these scale shapes for using slides:

And now let's check out some examples using these slides.

TRACK 79 · EXERCISE 21

TRACK 80 · EXERCISE 22

TRACK 81 · EXERCISE 23

TRACK 82 · EXERCISE 24

STRUMMING

Aside from the typical strumming patterns that you've most likely worked on already, there are a few other elements of strumming that come into play when learning a solo arrangement. Let's take a look at a few of them now.

MUTING NOTES WITH THE FRET HAND

Oftentimes, we'll need to strum through all four strings but we don't want four different notes sounding. There are a few different reasons for this, but they all basically involve muting one or more strings with the fret hand.

The non-adjacent triad voicings we learned in Chapter 4 are a prime example of this. Take the following root-position voicing on strings 4–2–1, for instance. When strumming it, you want to make sure that string 3 does not ring out.

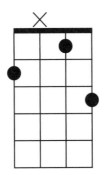

How do you do this? It's pretty simple, actually. Just let the underside of your middle finger (on string 4) and/or the tip of your index finger (on string 2) lightly touch string 3 to deaden it. (I actually think it's easier to do this than it is to let string 3 ring out on this chord, but maybe that's just my lazy fret-hand technique!)

This way, you'll be able to strum away on these chords and not worry about any wrong notes sneaking out. Try these next two examples to make sure you've got the feel of this technique.

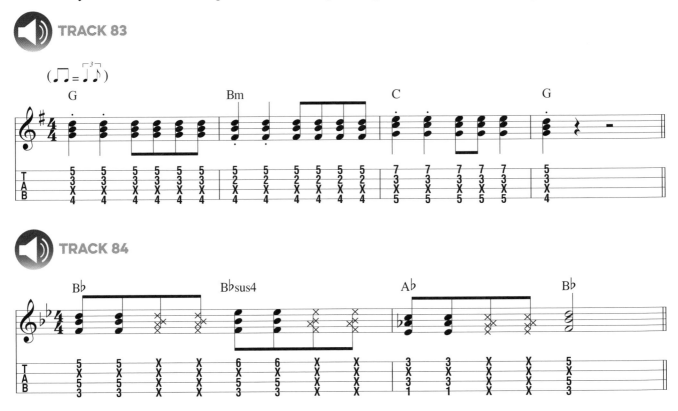

Another time when you'll need to use this technique is when you want to mute the top note of a chord, which is usually on string 1, so that the note on string 2 or string 4 (usually whichever is higher-pitched) will ring out as the melody. In these instances, you can use the same idea (muting string 1 with the underside of the finger on string 2) or you can simply release some pressure on string 1 while still maintaining some contact so that the string is silent and doesn't ring out. The following two examples demonstrate this idea.

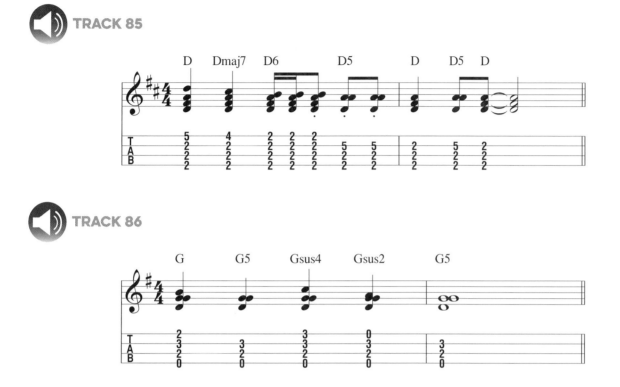

ROLLING A CHORD TO HIGHLIGHT A NOTE

Oftentimes, especially in slower tunes, it's a nice effect to roll through the chord and really highlight the melody note, which is usually (though not always) on string 1. I prefer to use the fleshy part of my thumb (not the nail) for this type of thing because:

1. I have greater dynamic control with the thumb during a strum.

2. I find the mellower tone pleasing, especially on ballads.

This is fairly easy to do, and it sounds great. Just think of the strum as a grace note and the final note (last note of the strum) as the target note. This means that you'll usually start the strum a bit earlier than you would a normal quick strum, but you can also land on the target note a little bit after the beat to create a more rubato feel.

Try it out with the example below, in which all of the melody notes are on string 1. Note, however, that the roll technique is only used on a few key spots.

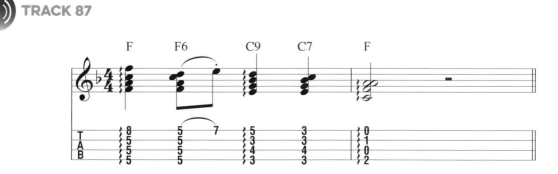

You can also use this technique to fool the ear a bit. Usually, our ears are apt to hear the highest note in a chord as the melody. This is why we usually arrange songs so that the melody is mostly on string 1. However, our ears are also drawn to the last note of a strum. So, we can use that, along with our roll technique, to bring out a melody note that's not the highest-pitched. In this next example, we're rolling through chords on strings 4–2 with our thumb, but we're bringing out the note on string 2 as the melody, even though the notes on string 4 are higher in pitch.

 TRACK 88

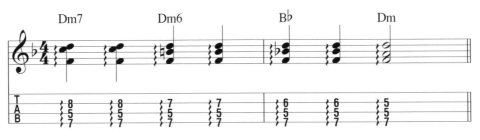

As a simple exercise of this idea, take the various chords below and strum through them with your thumb, first through all four strings, then strings 4–2, and finally, through only strings 4–3. Each time you strum, aim to highlight the last note of the strum, which should sound as the melody note even if it's not the highest-pitched in the chord.

TREMOLO

In case you don't already know, *tremolo* is the rapid strumming of a chord (or notes) for a period of time. Think of the Italian music you hear at a nice restaurant, and now think of what the mandolin is doing. Most likely it's playing a melody or chords with the tremolo technique.

A rousing tremolo strum on the final chord with the uke is a nice way to end an energetic arrangement, so it's really nice to have a good tremolo technique in your bag of tricks. Unfortunately, there's not one standard method for tremolo strumming; different people do it different ways, and you'll most likely need to experiment with a few different methods until you find something that works for you. Here are some things to keep in mind:

- Most people prefer to strum from the wrist, as opposed to the forearm, when tremoloing.

- Aim for a uniform sound in which the downstrokes are equal in volume to the upstrokes.

- Experiment with different angles of the strumming finger or thumb to help achieve a smooth, even sound.

- Ideally, you want to develop the ability to play quiet and loud tremolos so you can choose a stylistically appropriate one at the right time. This may mean strumming more quietly or using an entirely different technique (i.e., an index-finger strum for loud, raucous tremolo, and a thumb strum for quiet, mellow tremolo).

Whichever method you choose, make sure that you're not tensing up or tiring quickly. There may be times when you'll need to maintain the technique for several bars or more. Below are two examples of the tremolo technique. In the first example, I'm strumming with my index finger (which is held somewhat steady by my thumb) for a loud, brash sound. In the second example, I'm strumming with my thumb for a mellow, quieter sound. In both cases, I'm strumming with a wrist motion.

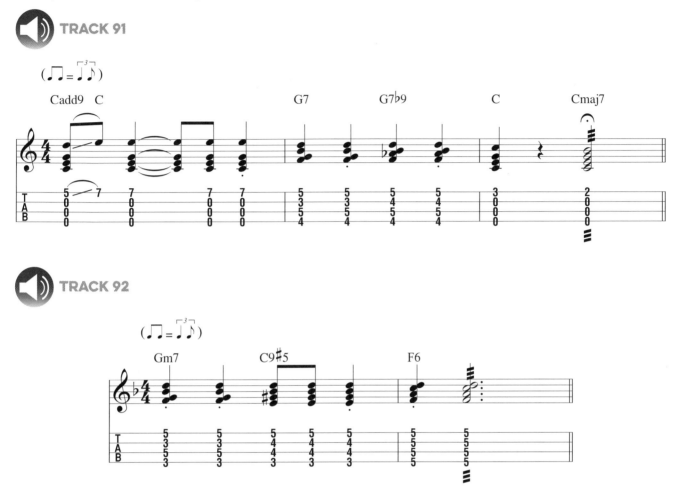

FINGERPICKING

If you haven't messed around with fingerpicking much yet, I'd recommend getting familiar with some standard patterns before tackling the arrangements. It's a great technique to have in your arsenal and can really open up the arranging possibilities. Most fingerpicking patterns fall into two main categories: *arpeggios* and *Travis picking*. Let's take a look at both styles. For each example, we'll label the plucking-hand fingers with the letters assigned in the guitar world, which are derived from Spanish:

- *p* = thumb
- *i* = index
- *m* = middle
- *a* = ring

ARPEGGIO PATTERNS

For these patterns, you generally assign one plucking-hand finger to one string. For example, if the pattern uses all four strings, it's common to just assign *p* to string 4, *i* to string 3, *m* to string 2, and *a* to string 1. For example, on the next page are some four-string patterns that use this concept. With the high G tuning, these patterns can sometimes feel a little counterintuitive, as we'd generally expect the thumb to be plucking the lowest note. However, this can be used to our advantage at times.

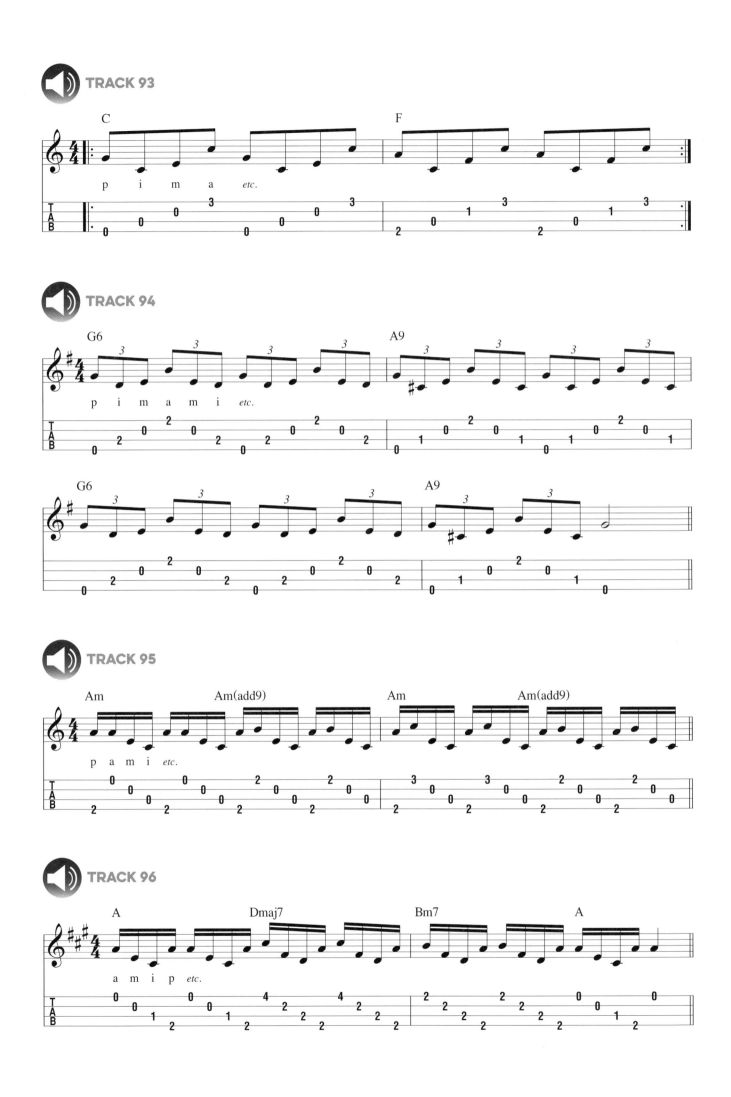

If you're only playing on strings 3–1, however, you may want to use *p* for string 3 and then *i* and *m* for strings 2 and 1, respectively.

TRACK 97

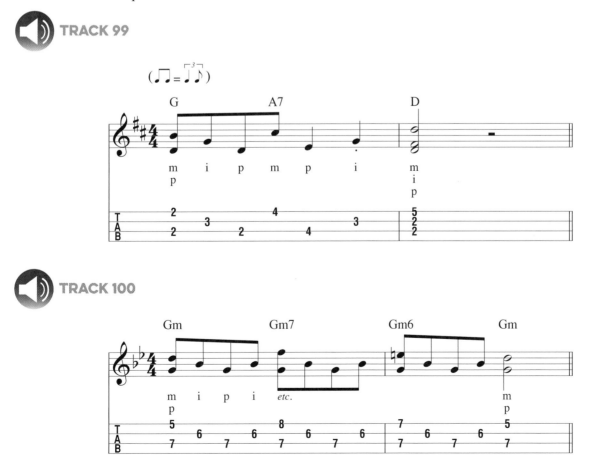

TRACK 98

In solo playing, these patterns may often involve the technique of *pinching*, which simply means playing two notes at the same time. This usually involves the thumb and a finger, but not always. Here are some examples of this idea:

TRACK 99

TRACK 100

TRAVIS PICKING

The Travis picking technique is named after country legend Merle Travis, who pioneered the style on guitar in the '30s and '40s. It was adopted and expanded upon by many players afterwards, most notably Chet Atkins, and now the name generally applies to a style in which the thumb alternates between two lower strings while the fingers fill in notes on top with the higher strings. Again, the reentrant tuning makes this interesting on the uke.

Let's take a look at an open C chord and see how this works. There are two basic approaches you can take with this style on the uke: you can start the thumb on string 4 or start it on string 3. While starting on string 4 may feel more natural (especially if you're a guitar player), starting on string 3 will generally *sound* more natural because the lowest note of the chord will appear on beat 1 instead of beat 2. However, both methods can certainly be useful at times, so there's no reason to stick to only one. Here are two basic patterns featuring these techniques. Notice that the thumb will rock back and forth between strings 4 and 3, and the *i* and *m* fingers will handle strings 2 and 1, respectively.

This rocking of the thumb back and forth is the backbone of the technique, and from there you can create numerous variations by alternating the order of the fingers, omitting notes, etc. Here are a few possible variations:

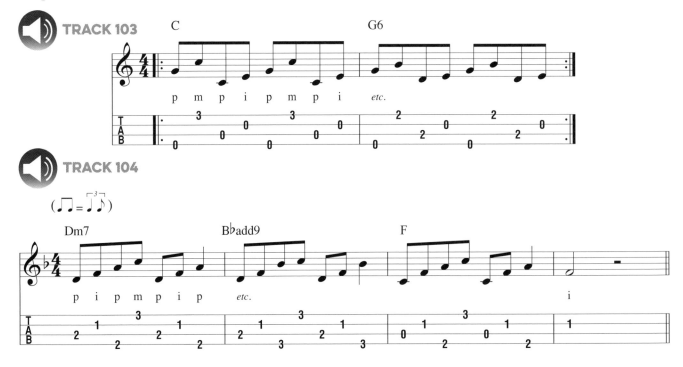

As with the arpeggio technique, we commonly employ pinching in Travis picking patterns when playing solo arrangements. The thumb is still the rock here and is usually holding down the fort by alternating back and forth on the beat.

Ideally, you should have these patterns down pat so that your thumb feels as though it's on auto-pilot. Occasionally, depending on the arrangement, you may break the pattern momentarily but, generally speaking, if it's a Travis picking pattern, that thumb is rocking back and forth like Granny Smith in her rocking chair.

DOUBLE STOPS

A *double stop* is simply two notes played at the same time. You may also hear them called *dyads* (the two-note version of triads). These little two-note wonders can be a great device to use in your arrangements when you want a melody to stand out in a different way than perhaps it did in an earlier section. You're essentially harmonizing a melody note with one at a set interval. The most common intervals used in double stops are 3rds and 6ths, but you'll occasionally see 4ths and 5ths, as well. Although 2nds and 7ths aren't out of the question, they're rarely used in parallel motion like the other intervals are.

So, how do they work? Well, let's start with 3rds since they're the most common of all. We'll start by playing the F major scale along string 2.

Now we'll add notes to string 1 a 3rd higher. This is basically like playing an F major scale on string 1 from A to A.

When we play them together, we get double stops in 3rds. Notice that some of them are major 3rds (four half steps), while others are minor 3rds (three half steps). Regarding the fret-hand fingering for these, there are two obvious choices: either use your index finger for all the notes on string 1 (except for the open string) and your middle or ring finger on string 2, or use your ring finger for all the notes on string 2 and alternate your index and middle on string 1.

TRACK 107

3rds in F Major

Regarding the plucking hand, you have several options. The most common method (and the one I used for Track 107 above) is to simply brush down through the strings with your thumb. As long as you're not playing them too quickly, this method usually works great and sounds nice, too. Another nice option in this regard is to pluck them simultaneously with the *i* and *m* fingers.

SPEEDY DOUBLE STOPS

If you have to play 16th notes or faster, you can use a mini-strum motion with either the thumb or the index finger. It might take some work to get a feel for it, but it's certainly doable. When doing this, I employ plenty of fret-hand muting so that the surrounding strings don't ring out. For example, for the first double stop (F and A on strings 2 and 1), I would fret the F note with my index finger and then lay my middle finger lightly across strings 3 and 4 to keep them quiet. For the next one (G and Bb), I would again use my middle finger to deaden strings 3 and 4. When I get to Bb and D in fifth position, I would fret Bb with my ring, D with my middle, and lay my index finger across strings 3 and 4 to keep them quiet, etc.

Don't forget that you can also use string 4 instead of string 1 to play the same 3rd double stops. It will sound slightly different because the G string is thinner than the A string, but sometimes it works out better to do so in certain arrangements.

Double stops in 6ths are another common interval. Below are 6ths in F major played on strings 3 and 1. We're basically playing an F major scale from C to C on string 3 and an F major scale from A to A on string 1.

 **TRACK 108**

6ths in F Major

Here's what parallel 4ths in F sound like. We're on strings 2 and 1 here; watch out for the one A4 interval!

 **TRACK 109**

4ths in F Major

And, finally, here are 5ths in F major, also on strings 2 and 1. Watch out for the single d5 interval!

 **TRACK 110**

5ths in F Major

The 5ths are also easily accessible on strings 4 and 3 by barring with one finger (unless it's a d5).

TRACK 111

CHAPTER 6
MELODIC CONSIDERATIONS

Although the uke is one charming and awesome musical instrument, it has one Achilles' heel with regard to solo arrangements when compared to others: range. Compared to a guitar, for example, which sports three-and-a-half octaves, we have basically half the range. And don't even mention a piano. Therefore, we're often required to rework some melodies in order to make them playable on the instrument. There are other factors that will come into play that require some tweaking, as well, depending on what exactly we're trying to do with a particular song. In this chapter, we'll look at these issues and suggest ways around them. These are the types of decisions you'll need to make when necessary so that the arrangement is playable while still sounding convincing. It often comes down to choosing what the most important element of the song is that you need to highlight.

RANGE OF THE MELODY

This is the first thing to look at. We basically have a little more than one octave with which to work on string 1, which is where we'd ideally like to place the melody notes most of the time (this is certainly not a steadfast rule, however). This means that, if a melody spans much more than an octave (and many do), we'll likely need to do something in order to create a playable arrangement, including one or more of the following:

- Selecting the appropriate key for the uke arrangement.
- Transposing certain sections or phrases of the melody up or down an octave as necessary.
- Play parts of the melody unaccompanied or with double stops.
- Omit parts of the melody.

Some songs will lend themselves to arrangements better than others. Generally speaking, you're looking for songs that have a well-established melody as opposed to just a loose, bluesy, and largely improvised melody.

Let's have a look at "The Star Spangled Banner" as an example. The first thing we need to do is examine the melody and find its range. When doing so, we find that it spans an octave plus a 5th. The first "say" is the lowest note of the melody (the tonic), and the climactic "free" toward the end is the highest note (the 5th above the octave). Knowing this, and if we want to keep the melody in its normal range throughout (which would be nice so that the climax is, in fact, climactic), we can probably eliminate the keys of G major through B major right off because the lowest G note is here:

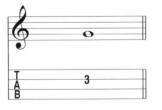
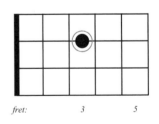

And that would put the high D note (the 5th) way up here:

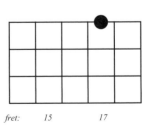

Which is too high.

I like to try to stay at or below fret 12 when I can. If fret 12 on string 1 were the highest note, that would be A, which would put the song in the key of D. That's a possibility. But since a C note is the lowest note we can play, and it's the lowest note of the melody, let's just go ahead and put it in C major. This will also open up the possibility of using some more open strings if we want to.

So, here's one possibility for playing the melody in the key of C major:

TRACK 112 **The Star Spangled Banner**

Words by Francis Scott Key
Music by John Stafford Smith

Since this song isn't a pop song (i.e., it doesn't have a "groove" beneath it or anything), it's often harmonized in "part-writing" fashion. In other words, you often see it arranged in two-part or three-part harmony. And since we don't need to be strumming chords beneath it, we can take the liberty of using up almost the entirety of the uke's range for the melody. Here's a sample of what a common approach would be in duet style:

TRACK 113 # The Star Spangled Banner

Words by Francis Scott Key
Music by John Stafford Smith

Note that we've made use of the open G string at times to double a melody note (measures 4, 7, and 16) and at other times because it simply made the phrase easier (measures 12 and 20). Also note the 3rds harmony in measures 9–11, which is just like we saw in Chapter 5 (only this time it's in C major instead of F major).

When dealing with pop songs, however, the range is more of an issue because we usually want to be supplying some accompaniment to the melody. This is why we like to keep the melody on string 1 if we can. Depending on the song, various approaches could work best. And when we say "depending on the song," we're talking about a range of factors, including one or more of the following:

- Style and tempo of the song.

- Speed and contour of the melody.

- Rhythmic complexity of the melody or chords.

For example, if you have a fairly easy melody in F major that spans from this A to this D in the verse section:

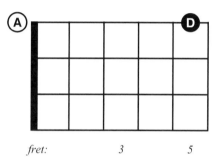

But then spans from this F to this A in the chorus:

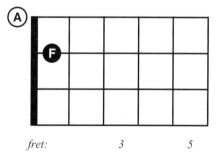

You may want to transpose the chorus melody up an octave so you have more options at your disposal for the chords beneath it, etc.

COMPLEXITY

If the song is complex rhythmically, harmonically, or melodically, it will obviously affect what you can do with it. Some melodies are hard enough to play by themselves, much less harmonize with chords at the same time. In these instances, you need to find what you consider crucial and work around it. For example, let's say you've got a song in C minor with a funky little melody like this:

After deciding that the rhythm of this melody is king, you decide that you can't change that. The key lays out nicely, so we can leave it in C minor. But we've got to find out how to: A) play the melody while, B) adding the chords below it.

First, we find a spot where the melody lays nicely on the fretboard, such as this, which is mostly in third position:

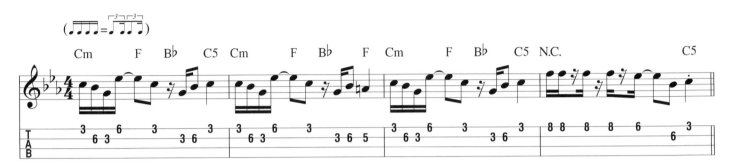

At this point, we need to start adding chords beneath melody. Don't worry too much about having to play them together; just try to find a spot where both parts can exist. We need a Cm chord, an F chord, and a B♭ chord. After some experimentation, I found these shapes for the Cm and F chords, which reside right near the melody:

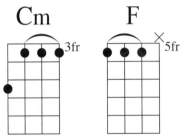

But I didn't like my options for B♭ around third position, so I decided to put the melody in first position at that point so I can use the B♭ chord there.

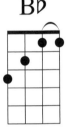

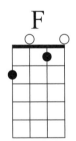

This works out nicely for the next phrase, as well. The melody ends on A, so I can use the open F chord and remain in first position.

The third phrase is a repeat of the first, so that just leaves the fourth phrase, which is kind of an ensemble run ("N.C." stands for "no chord") that the whole band would likely play together. On these types of things, octaves are always a good choice because it helps thicken the riff up. We can play octaves below all of these notes except the B♭, but we can at least get a double on it by playing string 4, as well.

Now that we've got a chord strategy, next we need to decide how to technically pull it off. For the melody, we can employ some pull-offs to make it easier. It's a good idea in more complicated arrangements like this to separate the parts so you can make sure each one is being represented accurately when they're put together. So, here's the melody by itself:

After experimenting with playing the chords and melody together, I decided that I can just leave off string 4 during the Cm and F chords and it sounds fine because we have the important chord tones covered. Plus, this also allows me to fret the F chord with my middle and ring fingers so that the melody notes (B♭ and G, played with pinky and index, respectively) can be sustained. This helps support the illusion of melody and accompaniment. So here's the accompaniment by itself:

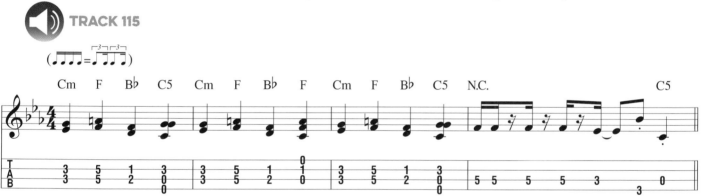

Regarding the plucking hand, there are several possibilities here. To increase the precision, I decided to fingerpick the first beat, using the fingering shown below, and then strum the chords with the thumb while using the fingers for the melody to help set them apart in tone. For the B♭ chord in beat 3, I found a happy accident for the melody whereby I can simply hammer from the chord's F note on string 2 to the G note at fret 3. At the last C chord of each measure, I decided to use the open C note on string 3 to get a deeper bass note. Even though there's no E♭ note here (the minor 3rd of Cm), it's implied by the tonality of the song and sounds fine to me. For the final octave run in measure 4, I strum it with my thumb and use careful fret-hand muting throughout. And now here's the final arrangement of this little ditty:

OTHER GENERAL GUIDELINES

Here are several other strategies that you can employ when dealing with difficult or troubling melodies. We'll see many of these ideas put to use in the arrangements in the next chapter.

SIMPLIFY THE RHYTHM

If a melody is just too syncopated to pull off while playing the accompaniment, you can often find ways to gently simplify it so that it's playable. Even moving one note by an eighth or 16th note can make all the difference sometimes. As long as the essence of the phrase is still there, adjustments like this are often negligible. This type of thing is purely a judgment call on your part, but there's no reason you can't experiment a bit if you come across something that's fighting you.

OMIT NOTES

Sometimes certain notes can simply be omitted because they're not terribly essential. A good candidate for this type of thing is, for example, a bluesy run that a singer may tag onto the end of a phrase. A good rule of thumb in this regard is the following: if it sounds as though it was probably improvised when it was recorded, then it's probably not terribly essential to the arrangement.

MAKE USE OF EVERYTHING YOU'VE GOT AVAILABLE

Don't forget that open strings can be a real lifesaver sometimes. Instead of having to fret a difficult 16th-note line, for example, maybe you can employ an open string at some point and make it a relatively easy finger-picked arpeggio pattern by mixing fretted notes with open strings. The same can be said of the fourth string. With the fourth and first strings being only a major 2nd away from each other, there are plenty of opportunities for sneaking in the fourth string during a quick melody, possibly easing the burden on your plucking hand.

MIX IT UP

In songs with vocals, you have the benefit of different lyrics to help maintain interest and put a new spin on a familiar melody. With solo arrangements, though, we have to rely on other methods to create interest. Therefore, if you're creating an arrangement of a song in which several sections are repeated, consider mixing things up and treating the melody differently in one of the repeats to help maintain interest. Use your imagination. Depending on the song, numerous approaches will work. You can bring the dynamics way down and streamline the arrangement to just a melody with minimal accompaniment. You can employ double stops to harmonize the melody. Or maybe you could switch from a strumming approach to a Travis picking approach, etc. Sometimes all it takes is a change in timbre (use your thumb instead of your index finger) or dynamics (play very quietly, etc.). The options are many!

BE FLEXIBLE

As I've mentioned before, every song is unique. Sometimes every line of a song will fit perfectly within an arrangement plan you've chosen but one. Rather than killing yourself by trying to force-feed the phrase to your hands, try to keep the bigger picture in mind: you're arranging the song to play for people to hear. They want to recognize the melody; that's the main thing. People can fill in details on their own if you give them enough to go on. So, if you have the bassline, chords, and melody all going in that amazing arrangement of yours, and you just can't make it work without dropping that one note of the bass line, don't beat yourself up over it. You'd probably be surprised to hear how much this happens in your favorite uke arrangements. You're probably not always hearing *everything* you think you're hearing!

In this final chapter, we're going to see how all of these tools can be applied in real-world arrangements of several popular songs. These will range in difficulty and style, but I'll try to cover the bases so that we're applying just about everything we've talked about in some capacity. I'd recommend listening to the audio demonstrations of these first (while following along with the music) before trying to tackle them so you have an idea of what you're aiming towards. Most importantly, have fun with these!

TRACK 117

This Land Is Your Land

Words and Music by Woody Guthrie

Moderately

Chorus

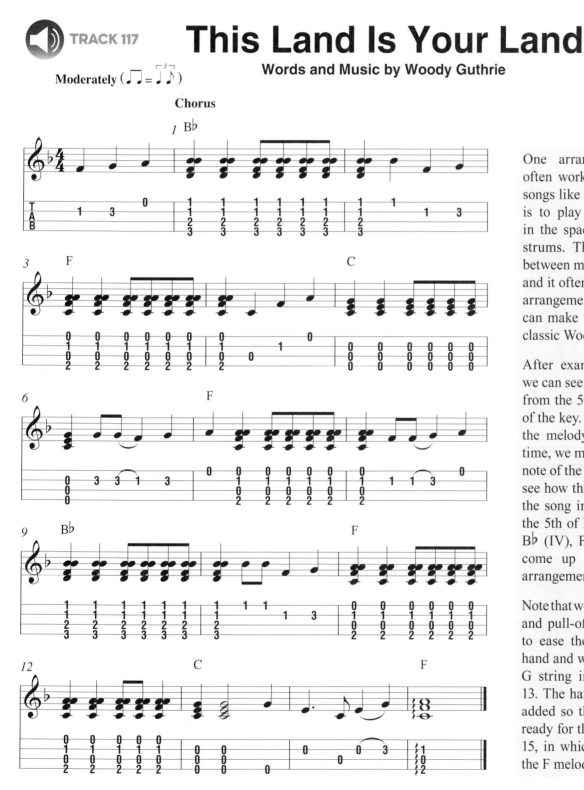

One arrangement strategy, which often works nicely on older pre-war songs like "This Land Is Your Land," is to play the melody and then fill in the spaces between it with chord strums. This is a nice compromise between melody and accompaniment, and it often results in a very effective arrangement. Let's look at how we can make use of this concept in this classic Woody Guthrie song.

After examining the vocal melody, we can see that it spans a minor 7th—from the 5th of the key up to the 4th of the key. Since we won't be playing the melody and chords at the same time, we may as well make the lowest note of the song the open C string and see how that works out. That will put the song in the key of F major (C is the 5th of F), and our chords will be Bb (IV), F (I), and C (V). We may come up with something like the arrangement shown here.

Note that we've employed hammer-ons and pull-offs at times in the melody to ease the burden on the plucking hand and we've made use of the open G string in the melody in measure 13. The hammer-on in measure 14 is added so that the pluck hand can be ready for the rolled strum in measure 15, in which you need to accentuate the F melody note on string 2.

Blue Skies

from BETSY
Words and Music by Irving Berlin

The lovely standard "Blue Skies" makes for an excellent and fun arrangement. The melodic range isn't too drastic, as it spans a major 6th—from the 5th of the key up to the major 3rd—so several keys are possibilities in that regard. I chose the key of B♭ major (or G minor), because it allowed me to stay fairly low on the neck and still get good separation.

For this song, I really wanted to try to separate the melody and chords so that it gives the illusion of two different instruments. So I decided to play the melody as normal but only have the chords play on the backbeats (beats 2 and 4). Whereas the melody is sustained throughout for the most part, the chords are clipped, which automatically helps to create the illusion of two separate instruments. This arrangement is also a perfect example of what I referred to at the end of Chapter 6 under the "Be Flexible" section. Although it sounds as though I'm playing two-note chords on beats 2 and 4 throughout, that's not always the case. Check out measures 2 and 4 for evidence of this. The melody encroaches upon the chord's space (string 2), but it's hardly noticeable at all because it simply takes the place of the chord's note and it works anyway.

I've added my fingerings for both hands throughout here, because some of it can be a little tricky. Feel free to alter it if you wish, but this should be a good starting point. One of the big challenges here is to sustain the melody while keeping the chords staccato (most of the time). For this reason, I play the entire chorus section with a *p-i-m-a* finger assignment (*p* on 4, *i* on 3, *m* on 2, *a* on 1) exclusively, as

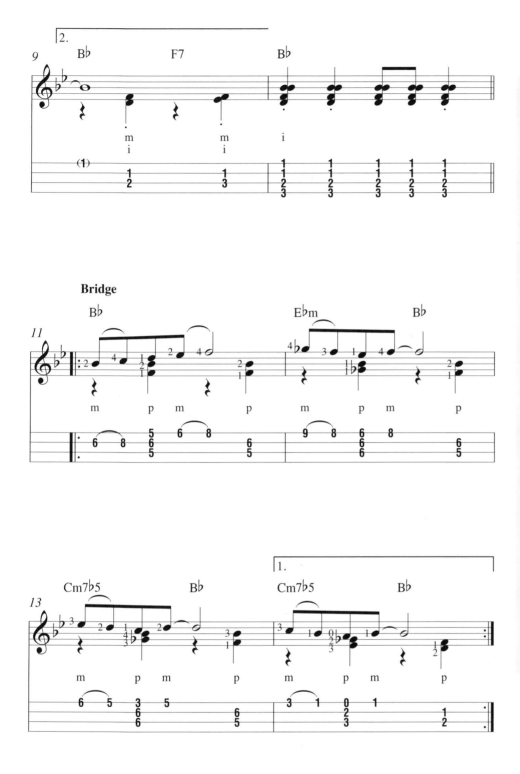

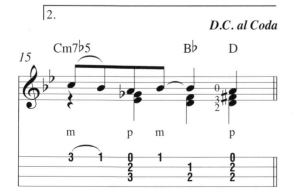

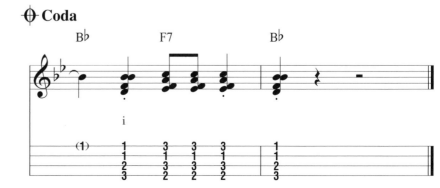

it allows me total control with regards to muting strings when necessary. In this case, this means muting the chords immediately after you play each one. So, for example, after playing the first open G string in measure 1, you play the chord on strings 3 and 2 with *i* and *m* and then immediately replant those fingers on the strings to mute them. On beat 3, you play the high D melody note on string 1 with the *a* finger and then play the chord on strings 3 and 2 again, *while leaving string 1 sustaining*, and then mute the chord immediately afterward again. This idea of leaving the melody note sustained while clipping the chords below happens throughout the chorus section, so take your time with it.

In the bridge, I soften up the chords a bit by simply strumming through them with the thumb to help set the sections apart. As such, it worked nicely for me to simply alternate the *m* finger for the melody notes and the thumb for the chord strums, but feel free to adjust this if you'd like. Note the use of hammer-ons and pull-offs here to help with the speedier eighth notes in the melody. The beginning of measure 13 is particularly tricky for the fret hand, so pay close attention to the fingerings and work it up slowly.

Beyond the Sea

Lyrics by Jack Lawrence
Music by Charles Trenet and Albert Lasry
Original French Lyric to "La Mer" by Charles Trenet

Moderate Swing (♩♩ = ♩♪)

Verse

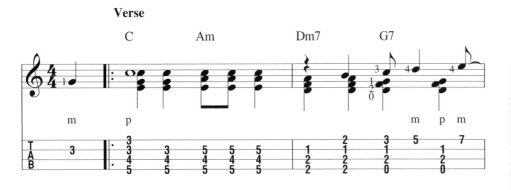

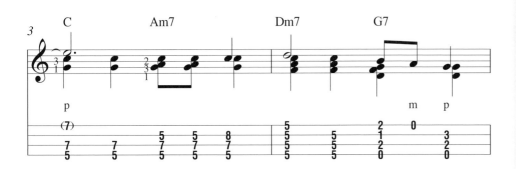

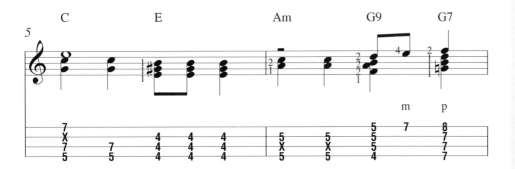

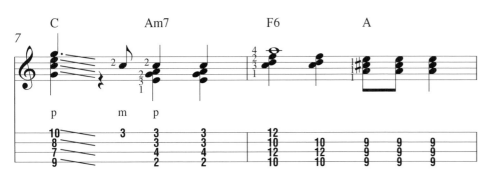

"Beyond the Sea" is a nice jazz pop standard song popularized by Bobby Darrin in 1959 and covered by numerous artists since. It's got fairly typical jazz changes, including I–vi–ii–V patterns and other common elements. The vocal melody spans an octave and a 2nd, from the low 5th up to the high 6th of the key. Since I wanted to treat this with a jazz style, access to open position wasn't a concern, because most jazz comping (on guitar, for example) doesn't make use of open strings. This is because the chords—quarter-note chords, for example—are often not sustained for their full duration, falling somewhere between staccato and legato. This is easier to do when you're not using open strings because you can simply stop them by releasing pressure on your fret hand. Needless to say, we'll be using a lot of the chord forms we learned in Chapter 4! So if you don't have those down, go refresh your memory before tackling this arrangement. I chose the key of C for this tune, which put the highest melody note at fret 12 of string 1, which is about as high as I like to ever go.

Regarding the plucking hand, since I was going for a warmer jazz tone, I mostly strummed the strings with the thumb throughout. When I needed notes in between the chord strums, which were mostly quarter notes in the "Freddie Green style" (rhythm guitarist for Count Basie), I usually plucked them with the *m* finger. So, in measure 1, for example, after the pickup note, which I plucked with the *m* finger, I simply brush through all four strings, accenting string 1 at the end of the strum to help bring out the melody

note. For the rest of the measure, I try to simply strum with my thumb on strings 4–2. However, I'm not too concerned if I happen to restrike string 1. I'm still holding that melody note down with my index finger, and if I happen to nick it with a thumb strum, it's negligible to the ear because it's part of the chord anyway. Couple this with the fact that the uke doesn't have a lot of sustain anyway, so it's hardly a crime. That's pretty much the approach I use for the entire arrangement: gentle thumb strums while trying to bring out the melody on string 1.

There are a few quick chord moves, as in measures 6 and 9, so take your time working those parts up. Again, I've included my fret-hand fingerings on the questionable parts throughout, so be sure to check them out if you're having trouble. Notice how, in measure 12, we roll the strum so as to accent the G melody note, which is below the B note on string 4.

All Apologies

Words and Music by Kurt Cobain

Next up we have a fun arrangement of Nirvana's "All Apologies." The original made use of a riff played against a droning open string, and so I've used that idea as the basis for this arrangement. After examining my potential in this regard on the uke, I chose the key of A, handling most of the melody on string 3 against the droning open second and first strings. I also played some melodies on string 2 against the droning open first string.

For the intro riff, I strummed with my thumb, doing my best to only strike strings 3 and 2 when playing the melody on string 3, and strings 2 and 1 when playing the melody on those strings. Fret-hand muting plays a key role here as well. For example, in measure 1, while playing the melody on string 3, I'm allowing my fret-hand finger to touch string 4 in order to keep it quiet, should I accidentally nick it with the thumb while strumming.

For the verse section, I move to a fingerpicking approach, again using the open second and first strings as drones to fill in the spaces around the melody. This creates a steady stream of eighth notes, which is the foundation of the song's rhythm in the original recording. Notice the variation in the third and fourth statements of the melody, where I add a harmony note a 3rd higher on string 1. Throughout this whole section, I pluck strings 3–1 with *p*, *i*, and *m*, respectively.

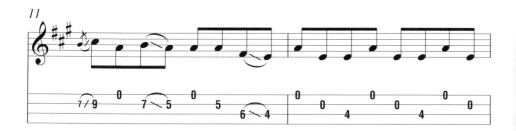

At the chorus, I move to a strumming approach with the *i* finger, keeping the melody on string 2 or 1. This is a perfect example of how sometimes the melody note can weave in and out of the chords with regard to the range. Sometimes it's the highest note of the chord, but other times it's not. I could have arranged it so that it was always the highest note, but it didn't seem to need it, as it was perfectly detectable this way. Not only that, but in measure 21, the brief minor 2nd interval created between the A note on string 4 (fret 2) and G# on string 2 (fret 4) is really beautiful. Notice the accent marks in the music (>), which tell you where to place the emphasis in your strumming. The pull-offs in measures 23 and 24 serve two purposes: 1) They help to accent those melody notes, and 2) They automatically silence string 1 (your finger will touch string 1 as it pulls off string 2), which helps ensure that the melody note is heard clearly. For the high C# notes on string 1 (fret 4) at the end of measures 22 and 25, fret with your pinky or ring finger and lay your index finger lightly across the other strings to mute them. This also perfectly prepares you for the barre that happens immediately afterward.

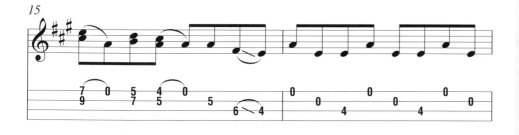

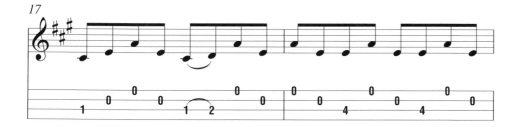

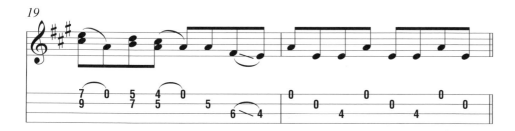

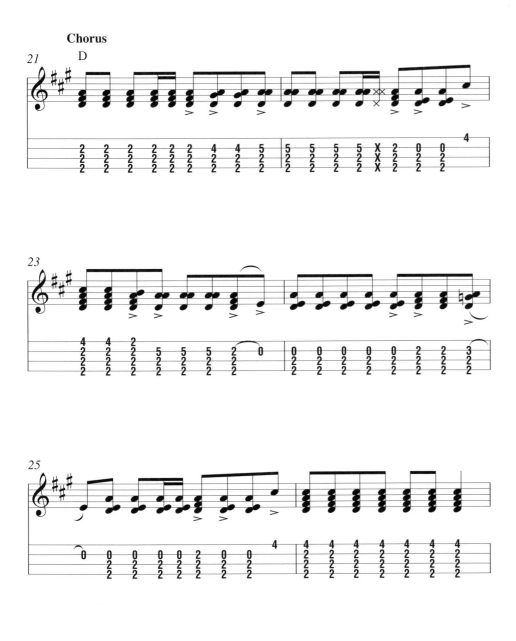

Chorus

In measure 28, tap the drum fill by slapping the body of your uke with your plucking hand. If you use two different spots—maybe on the side and on the face—you can kind of simulate a bass drum and snare. In measure 30, I specifically chose to play the final melody note (the G♯ note) at fret 8 on string 3 simply because it made it easier to execute a slide down the neck, which I wanted to do. For the outro melody ("All we are…"), we return to fingerpicking, using an altered Travis picking pattern. Use *p* for strings 4 and 3 here, *i* for string 2, and *m* for string 1. Don't miss the purposeful exploitation of the high G string at the end of measure 39 here. Not only does this make it easier for both hands, but it also allows you to ring the D and C♯ notes together for a bit if you'd like, which sounds very nice.

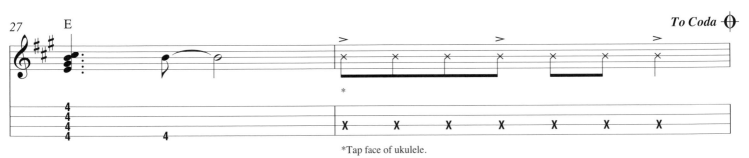

*Tap face of ukulele.

Coda

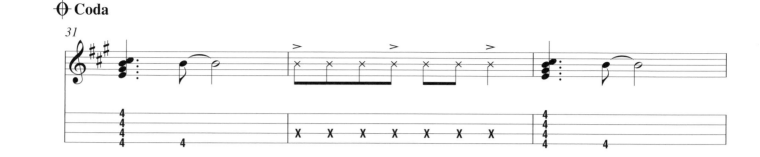

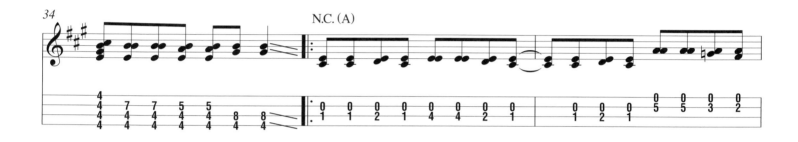

Outro

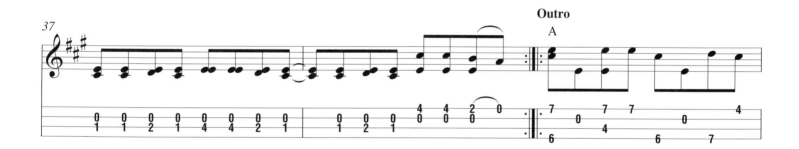

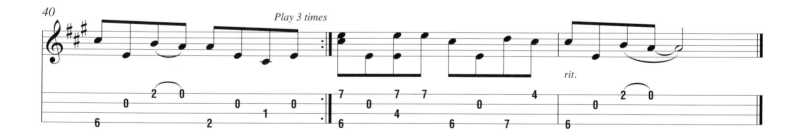

You Are So Beautiful

Words and Music by Billy Preston and Bruce Fisher

The tender '70s ballad "You Are So Beautiful" is one of Joe Cocker's signature songs and biggest hits. Here we treat it to a lovely chord-based arrangement in the key of A. The basic strategy was to strum chords on the beats, keeping the melody on the top string. During pauses between melodic phrases, I filled in the gaps with arpeggios from the chords.

Speaking of the chords, this song contains a lot of them, and some of them change pretty rapidly. I've included fingerings where I thought they'd be helpful. Of particular note is the main descending chord sequence of A–A–Amaj7–A7 that happens several times throughout the song. For the Amaj7 chord, I'm fretting string 4 (fret 2) with my index finger and string 1 (fret 4) with my pinky. Then I'm barring strings 3 and 2 at fret 4 with my ring finger. The reason for this, instead of simply barring strings 3–1 with my ring finger, is so that I don't have to lift my pinky off the melody note on string 1 for the whole sequence, resulting in a much more connected sound. If you try playing the Amaj7 with only the index finger and ring barre, I think you'll notice the difference. The melody gets clipped short both before and after the Amaj7 chord.

In measure 9, we make use of a harmonic on string 1 at fret 12 to avoid making a massive stretch. Measure 12, however, does feature a bit of stretching in beats 3 and 4—not to mention some sophisticated rhythms. If you have trouble hearing them, check out the audio track. This is a uke, though, so the stretch isn't too bad. Just be sure to prepare for it.

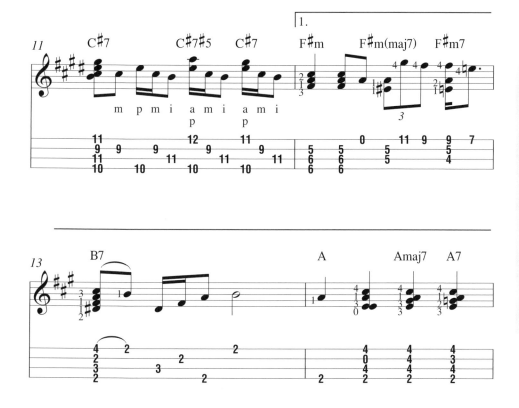

Regarding the plucking hand, I'm brushing through most of the chords here with the thumb for a gentle sound. When the arpeggios show up, I'm generally plucking them with *p* on strings 4 and 3 and *i* and *m* on strings 2 and 1, respectively, but I'll occasionally make an adjustment if it feels better. In measure 19, I'm using a reverse roll, from string 2 to string 4, because I really want the notes on string 4 to speak. Feel free to take a bit of liberty with the tempo on this piece if you'd like, as the rubato style suits this type of song well.

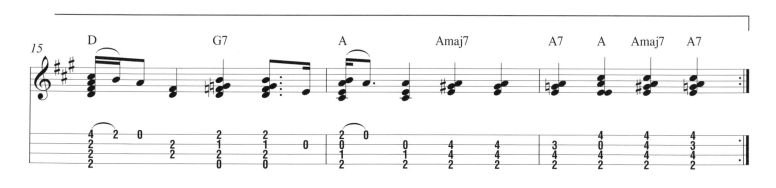

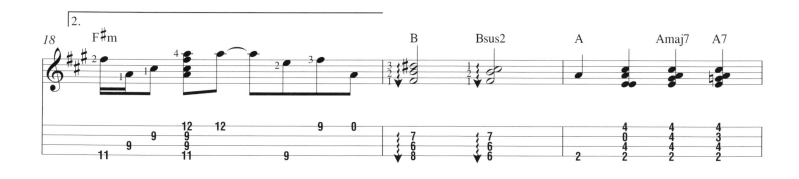

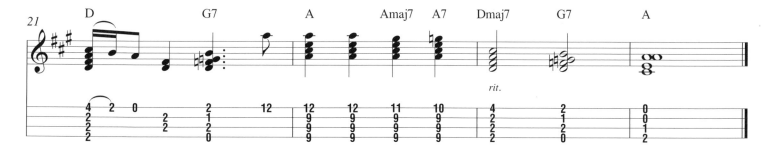

My Favorite Things

from THE SOUND OF MUSIC

Lyrics by Oscar Hammerstein II
Music by Richard Rodgers

No doubt a favorite moment for many from the musical *The Sound of Music*, "My Favorite Things" has endured for decades as a classic, always receiving a hefty share of airplay during the holidays. This arrangement treats the song to a swinging jazz feel, which suits the harmonic vocabulary of the song quite fittingly. The song is in 3/4, and I've arranged it in the key of B minor in order to accompany the wide range of the melody, which spans over an octave. Because this song has a lot of chords that change quickly (every bar for the most part) and an active melody, I've arranged it with one chord at the beginning of each measure followed by the melody. Anything more would result in something that sounds too busy, in my opinion (not to mention quite a handful). This also allows me to add a bit of character to the melody via slides in some places.

The intro, which vamps over the four-chord descending progression that begins the verse, can either be strummed with the thumb or the index finger. The latter will result in a slightly brighter tone, so experiment and see which sound you prefer. There are a number of ways to fret these chords, but I prefer to fret the first Bm with middle, index, and ring on strings 4–2, respectively. (This is because you'll need to use this fingering at the beginning of the verse anyway in order to use the pinky for the high F♯ note.)

At the verse, the primary M.O. of strumming a chord on beat 1 and continuing with melody begins. For this, I'm strumming with my thumb and plucking the following melody notes with either my index or middle finger.

By far the most troubling spot (for me) here is measure 6, the Bm(maj7) chord. There are two possible fingerings for it: pinky-middle-ring-index (strings 4–1) or ring-middle-middle-index (strings 4–1). As indicated in the music, I prefer the latter, which requires barring the middle finger on strings 3 and 2. This isn't terribly easy, because you have to make sure you're clearing string 1 as well. However, I found it easier than the alternative. Six one way, half a dozen the other.

In measure 7, try to roll your index finger slightly after the barre on beat 1 so that the chord doesn't bleed into the melody note that immediately follows on string 1. In other words, you'll be playing that B note at fret 2, string 1 about halfway down your first finger—not on the tip. This is known as a "hinge barre" in classical guitar. (Think of your first finger being attached to string 1 on a hinge.) If this is too difficult, you can fret the note on string 1 with your middle finger as an alternative. The sequence from measure 13 to 15 involves a lot of shifts and specific fretting, so take your time with it. Work it up slowly and cement the muscle memory before speeding it up. Also, watch out for the chromatic melody in measure 43. Notice that I use my pinky for the last note in this measure (F♯ at fret 9, string 1). This is just because it prepares me for the following chord, in which the pinky plays the high G note at fret 10. This isn't an easy arrangement, but it sounds great and is a lot of fun to play.

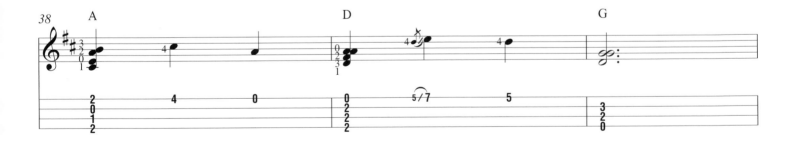

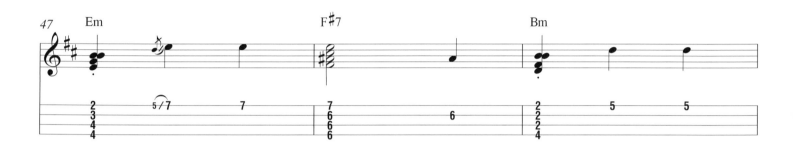

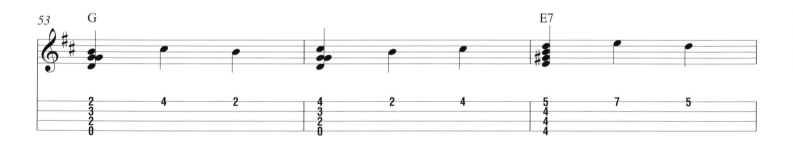

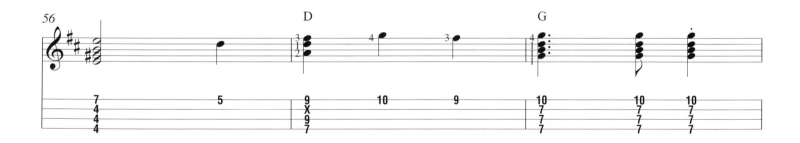

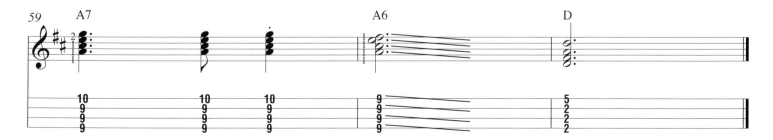

Annie's Song
Words and Music by John Denver

Next up we have a version of John Denver's beautiful ballad, "Annie's Song." This was a somewhat rare occurrence in which I was able to stick with the original key and style—i.e., a fingerpicked arrangement in D major. We're in 3/4 for this tune, and I used a kind of mutated Travis picking approach, usually alternating the thumb on each beat in a string 4–string 3–string 4 fashion, with the fingers adding the melody and filling in the gaps.

One exception to the above-mentioned routine happens in the intro, in which I'm playing a specific pattern to simulate John's guitar intro. Notice that the thumb here is playing string 3–string 4–string 4. Throughout the whole song, strings 1 and 2 are handled by the *m* and *i* fingers exclusively, save for a very few exceptions in which the melody features two eighth notes in a row played on the same string. In these instances—measures 7, 11, 15, 19, and 23—I alternate the *m* and *i* fingers for those two notes.

For the most part, the chord shapes fall under the fingers pretty well, but there are a few tricky spots here and there. I've included my preferred fingerings throughout when it wasn't obvious. When moving from the Bm chord to the G chord, which happens several times in the song, use a 3/4 barre for the Bm chord (i.e., barre only strings 3–1 at fret 2). This will allow you to leave that barre in place for the G chord that follows. In measure 31, notice that I take advantage of the open E (second) string for the last eighth note. This provides time to get in position for the following A chord, which is a bit tricky and requires a slight stretch.

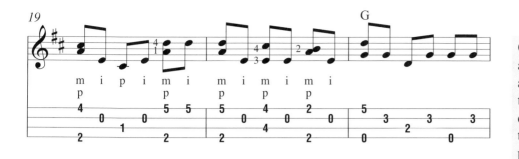

Overall, it's not a terribly difficult arrangement, yet it still sounds great and very much retains the essence of the original. To me, the most difficult aspect is remembering to break the string 4–string 3–string 4 thumb pattern when reaching measure 33, so be sure to watch out for that.

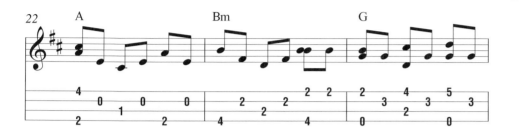

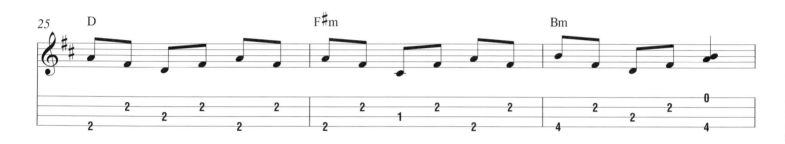

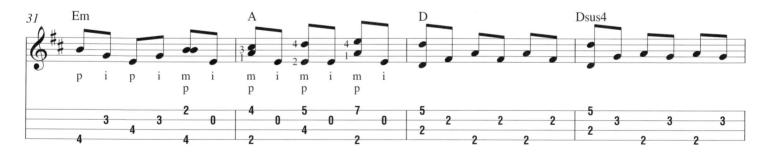

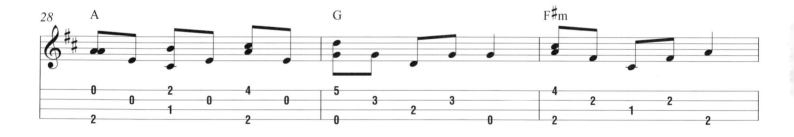

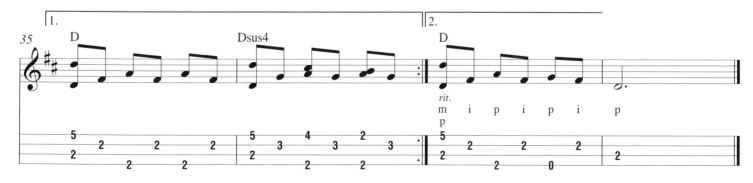

Blowin' in the Wind

Words and Music by Bob Dylan

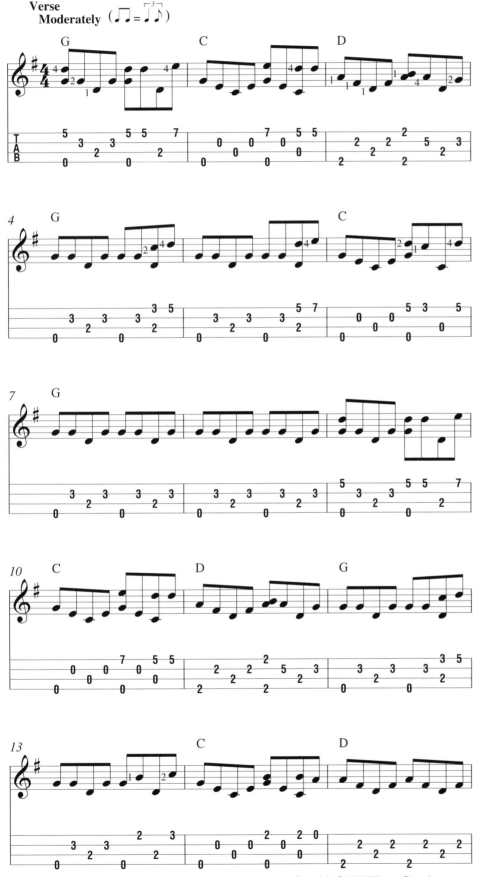

One of the most well-known folk songs of the 20th century, and an indisputable classic of Bob Dylan's catalog, "Blowin' in the Wind" makes for a lovely Travis-picking style arrangement on the uke. I went with the key of G for this one to take advantage of as many open strings as possible—not to mention the melody happened to fall nicely in open position (mostly).

For the most part, the plucking here is pretty consistent. The thumb is alternating between string 4 and 3 almost the whole time, and the *i* and *m* fingers are assigned to strings 2 and 1, respectively. There are a few exceptions to this. On several occasions, the melody note features two eighth notes in a row played on the same string. In these instances—such as in measures 1, 2, 4, etc.—I'm alternating the *m* and *i* fingers for the melody notes. The other big exception to this occurs in measure 30. Notice on beat 3 that the plucking hand shifts over a string group, with *m* on string 2 and *i* on string 3.

Most of the fret-hand fingerings I've given are meant to allow the melody notes to sustain their full duration, so be sure to take a look at them. Other than that, this is a pretty straightforward arrangement and not too difficult once you have the Travis-picking technique down. At the very end of the song, I use an artificial harmonic technique to add the sonic "cherry on top." First, fret the G note on string 2, fret 3 normally and, with your *plucking-hand index finger*, lightly touch the second string directly above the fret wire at fret 15 (12 frets above the fretted note). Then use your *plucking-hand ring finger* to pluck the string. You should get a chiming note that sounds just like

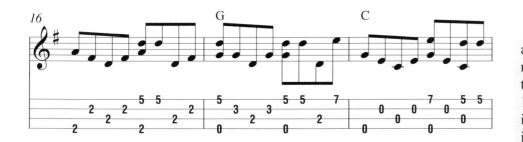

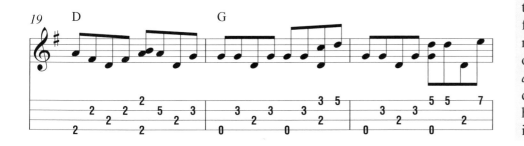

a 12th-fret (natural) harmonic, only a minor 3rd (three frets) higher. This is the same exact concept as a normal 12th-fret harmonic; i.e., we're dividing the string exactly in half. In this instance, though, our fretted note is acting as the nut, so half the length of the string is no longer at fret 12; it's 12 frets above the fretted note. Any harmonic that involves a fretted note (as opposed to an open string) is called an *artificial harmonic*. There are several different ways to produce artificial harmonics, and this specific technique is called a *harp harmonic*.

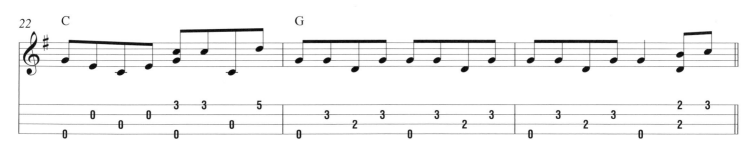

Chorus

To Coda ⊕

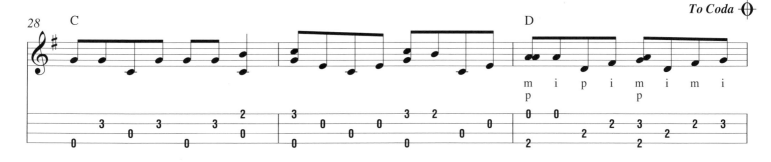

D.C. al Coda

⊕ **Coda**

Space Oddity

Words and Music by David Bowie

Intro
Slowly and gracefully

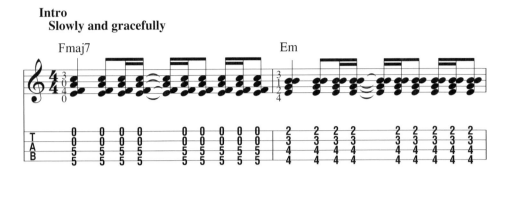

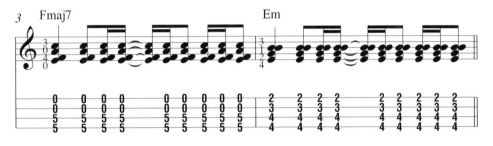

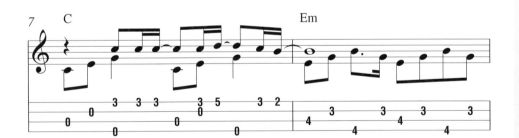

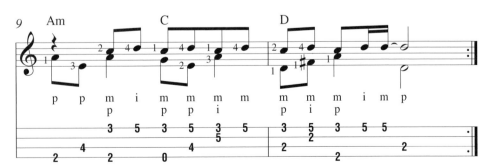

The late, great David Bowie's sprawling "Space Oddity" was the song that essentially launched his career in the early '70s. I've arranged this song in the original key of C major, as it lays out nicely on the uke. On a personal note, I had selected this song to arrange in December of 2015 just after starting this book. By the time I actually began to work out the arrangement, Bowie had tragically passed away in January of 2016. Therefore, I wanted to remain as true to his original as I could with this arrangement in tribute to him.

This is the final arrangement in this book because it's the most ambitious—not only in length, but also in technical challenges. There is a lot of separation between melody and chords (including contrasting rhythms), a mixture of textures (fingerpicking, strumming), and some tricky fret-hand fingerings. Most of the arrangement is split into two voices—chords are downstemmed, and the melody is upstemmed. Having said all that, it's not quite as hard as it may look (or sound) at first, as there is most often a basic formula at work.

After the strummed Fmaj7 and Em chords that kick off the song, we move to a very specific fingerpicking pattern for the latter half of the intro. The chords are outlined with arpeggios, while the melody is plucked above. As I mentioned earlier, I wanted to retain the true spirit of the original recording as much as possible, so I maintained nearly all of the syncopation in the vocal melody. This makes for a few sophisticated rhythms at times. I've included my preferred pluck-hand fingering throughout this section for your consideration. Basically, I use *p* for all the notes on strings 4 and 3, *i* for all

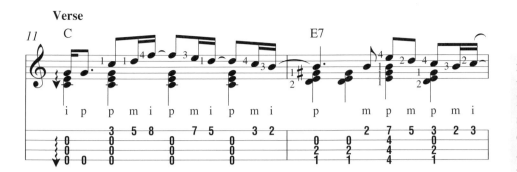

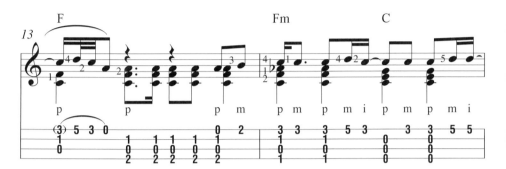

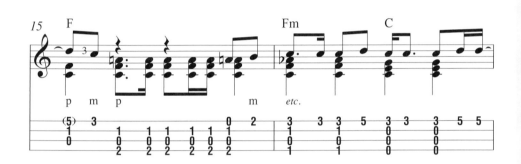

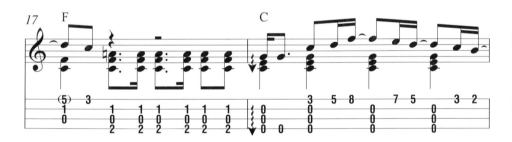

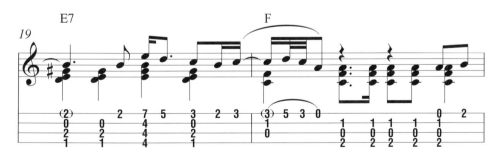

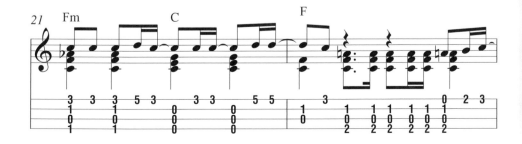

notes on string 2, and alternate *m* and *i* when necessary on string 1. Notice that I do bring the *a* finger in for one specific spot in measure 5. The tempo is slow enough here that I could have used *m* again for this note, but it's always good practice to alternate plucking fingers like this, because at faster tempos, repeating the same plucking finger will start to cause problems. This fingerpicking section will likely take a bit of effort to work up, but it's very beautiful when it comes together.

One of the reasons I used the delicate fingerpicking texture for the intro was to contrast it with the verse that follows, which blossoms so beautifully in the original recording. At this point, we move to the primary texture of the arrangement, which involves strumming chords with *p* and plucking the melody—usually on string 1—with *m* and *i*. One exception to this occurs right out of the gate at the beginning of measure 11. Because I wanted the G note to clearly be heard as the melody here, I rake across the strings (toward the ceiling) with *i* and immediately follow it with the open G string plucked by *p*. (It should be mentioned that I'm using one of my fret-hand fingers here to keep string 1 quiet.) From then on, melody notes that appear on the beat are strummed, along with the chord, by *p*, and the ones in between are plucked by *m* or *i*.

There are some tricky parts for the fret hand throughout, so I've included lots of suggested fingerings in that regard. One such instance that occurs several times is first seen in measure 14. It's a bit of stretch to reach up to the D note while holding the Fm chord below it, but I believe most people should be able to do it. If it's simply not possible, there is an alternative Fm voicing in third position, with F on string 3 (fret 5), A♭ on string 2 (fret 4), and C on string 1 (fret 3). In fact, I make use of this voicing, along with the open fourth string, in measure 23. This creates an Fm(add9) chord, which I used to help

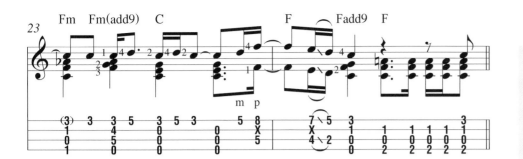

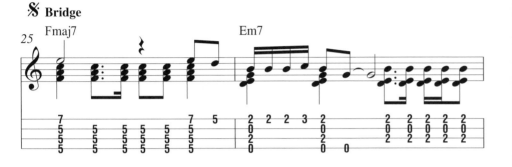

highlight the "stars look very different" lyric. At the end of that measure, I use octaves to really make the "today" climax stand out, resolving on beat 2 of measure 24 with a big-sounding Fadd9 chord. This maneuver will most likely take a bit of practice, but it's worth it.

The first chord of the interlude (measure 32) is not the easiest in the world. You have to be pretty precise and specific with your fret-hand position to get all those notes to speak. However, I wanted as big of a sound as I could manage for that riff (i.e., using all four strings), and I wanted the root notes to appear as the top voice, so that was my only option. One other tricky spot I'll mention happens first at the end of measure 12. In order to get in position for the little legato turn there, notice that I move to my middle finger for the very final C note. You have to reach back a little bit for the F note on string 2 (fret 1) at measure 13, but it makes the hammer/pull move much easier than if you'd used your ring finger.

Take your time with this one; there's a lot going on. But it's one of my favorite arrangements to play. I hope you enjoy it.

R.I.P. David.

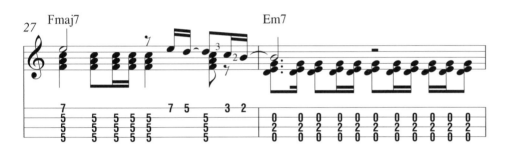

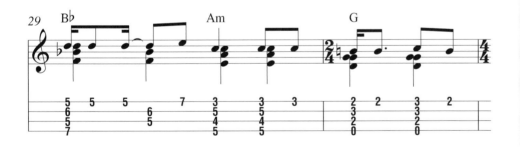

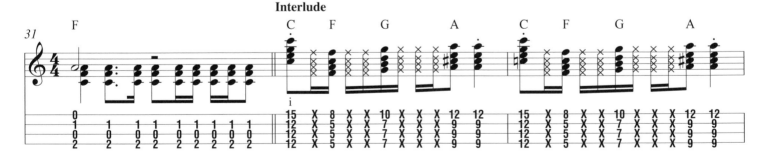

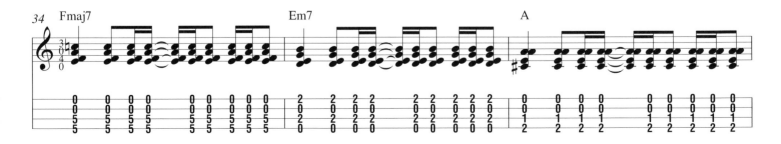

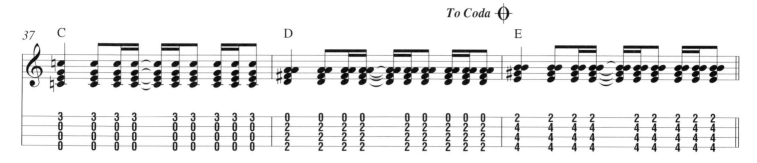

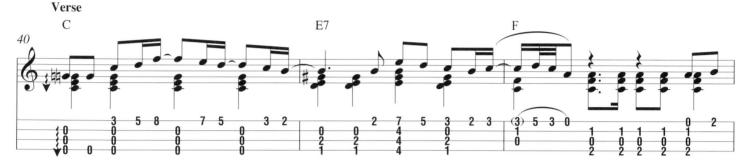

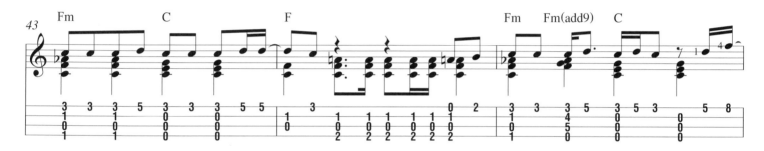

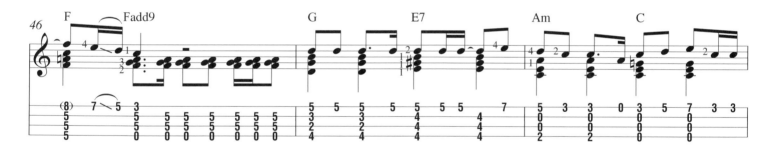

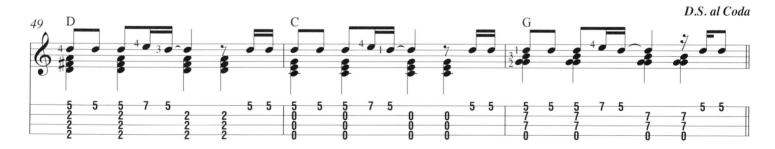

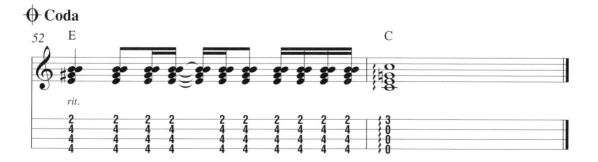

UKULELE NOTATION LEGEND

THE MUSICAL STAFF shows pitches and rhythms and is divided by bar lines into measures. Pitches are named after the first seven letters of the alphabet.

TABLATURE graphically represents the ukulele fingerboard. Each horizontal line represents a a string, and each number represents a fret.

Notes:

Strings:

2nd string, 3rd fret

1st & 2nd strings open, played together

open F chord

HALF-STEP BEND: Strike the note and bend up 1/2 step.

WHOLE-STEP BEND: Strike the note and bend up one step.

GRACE NOTE BEND: Strike the note and immediately bend up as indicated.

SLIGHT (MICROTONE) BEND: Strike the note and bend up 1/4 step.

BEND AND RELEASE: Strike the note and bend up as indicated, then release back to the original note. Only the first note is struck.

PRE-BEND: Bend the note as indicated, then strike it.

VIBRATO: The string is vibrated by rapidly bending and releasing the note with the fretting hand.

HAMMER-ON: Strike the first (lower) note with one finger, then sound the higher note (on the same string) with another finger by fretting it without picking.

PULL-OFF: Place both fingers on the notes to be sounded. Strike the first note and without picking, pull the finger off to sound the second (lower) note.

LEGATO SLIDE: Strike the first note and then slide the same fret-hand finger up or down to the second note. The second note is not struck.

SHIFT SLIDE: Same as legato slide, except the second note is struck.

TRILL: Very rapidly alternate between the notes indicated by continuously hammering on and pulling off.

TREMOLO PICKING: The note is picked as rapidly and continuously as possible.

NOTE: Tablature numbers in parentheses mean:

1. The note is being sustained over a system (note in standard notation is tied), or

2. The note is sustained, but a new articulation (such as a hammer-on, pull-off, slide or vibrato) begins, or

3. The note is a barely audible "ghost" note (note in standard notation is also in parentheses).

Additional Musical Definitions

 (accent)

- Accentuate note (play it louder)

 *(staccato)*

- Play the note short

D.S. al Coda

- Go back to the sign (𝄋), then play until the measure marked "*To Coda*," then skip to the section labelled "**Coda**."

D.C. al Fine

- Go back to the beginning of the song and play until the measure marked "*Fine*" (end).

N.C.

- No chord.

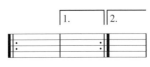

- Repeat measures between signs.

- When a repeated section has different endings, play the first ending only the first time and the second ending only the second time.